PRISM

READING AND WRITING   **3**

TEACHER'S MANUAL

Chris Sowton

Alan S. Kennedy

with
Wendy Asplin
Christina Cavage
Jeanne Lambert
Janet Gokay

CAMBRIDGE
UNIVERSITY PRESS

CAMBRIDGE
UNIVERSITY PRESS

University Printing House, Cambridge CB2 8BS, United Kingdom

One Liberty Plaza, 20th Floor, New York, NY 10006, USA

477 Williamstown Road, Port Melbourne, VIC 3207, Australia

4843/24, 2nd Floor, Ansari Road, Daryaganj, Delhi – 110002, India

79 Anson Road, #06–04/06, Singapore 079906

Cambridge University Press is part of the University of Cambridge.

It furthers the University's mission by disseminating knowledge in the pursuit of education, learning and research at the highest international levels of excellence.

www.cambridge.org
Information on this title: www.cambridge.org/9781316625194

© Cambridge University Press 2017

First published 2017
20 19 18 17 16 15 14 13 12 11 10 9 8 7 6 5 4 3 2 1

Printed in Malaysia by Vivar Printing

A catalogue record for this publication is available from the British Library

ISBN 978-1-316-62519-4 Teacher's Manual 3 Reading and Writing
ISBN 978-1-316-62445-6 Student's Book with Online Workbook 3 Reading and Writing

CONTENTS

SCOPE AND SEQUENCE

UNIT	WATCH AND LISTEN	READINGS	READING SKILLS	LANGUAGE DEVELOPMENT	
1 GLOBALIZATION _Academic Disciplines_ Cultural Studies / Sociology	Chinese Flavors for American Snacks	1: Turkish Treats (blog) 2: Changing Eating Habits in Italy (essay)	_Key Skills_ Making predictions from a text type Topic sentences _Additional Skills_ Understanding key vocabulary Using your knowledge Reading for main ideas Reading for details Identifying purpose and audience Making inferences Synthesizing	Academic alternatives to phrasal verbs Globalization vocabulary	
2 EDUCATION _Academic Disciplines_ Communications / Education	College Debt and Bankruptcy	1: College Majors: Business vs. Engineering (essay) 2: Distance Learning vs. Face-to-Face Learning (article)	_Key Skill_ Making inferences _Additional Skills_ Understanding key vocabulary Using your knowledge Reading for main ideas Reading for details Synthesizing	Education vocabulary Academic words	
3 MEDICINE _Academic Disciplines_ Health Sciences / Medicine	A New Way to Handle Allergies	1: The Homeopathy Debate (article) 2: Should Health Care Be Free? (article)	_Key Skill_ Annotating a text _Additional Skills_ Understanding key vocabulary Using your knowledge Skimming Reading for main ideas Reading for details Scanning to find key words Identifying opinions Making inferences Synthesizing	Medical vocabulary Academic vocabulary	
4 THE ENVIRONMENT _Academic Disciplines_ Ecology / Environmental studies	Population and Water	1: Disaster Mitigation (interview) 2: Combating Drought in Rural Africa: A Report (report)	_Key Skill_ Identifying cohesive devices _Additional Skills_ Understanding key vocabulary Predicting content using visuals Using your knowledge Skimming Reading for main ideas Reading for details Making inferences Synthesizing	Academic noun phrases Natural disaster vocabulary	

CRITICAL THINKING	GRAMMAR FOR WRITING	WRITING	ON CAMPUS
Providing supporting examples Using tables and diagrams	Noun phrases Time phrases	*Academic Writing Skills* Essay structure Writing an effective thesis statement *Rhetorical Mode* Explanatory *Writing Task* How has globalization changed your country? (essay)	*Study Skill* Maximizing concentration levels
Using a Venn diagram to plan a comparison and contrast essay Analyzing similarities and differences	Comparison and contrast language: • Transitions to show comparison and contrast • Adverb clauses of contrast	*Academic Writing Skills* Avoiding run-on sentences and comma splices Comparison and contrast essays *Rhetorical Mode* Comparison and contrast *Writing Task* Discuss the various similarities and differences between studying a language and studying math. (essay)	*Communication Skill* Class discussion boards
Evaluating and analyzing ideas	Articles: • Definite article (*the*) • Indefinite article (*a/an*) • No article (Ø) • Articles in discourse Transitions to show concession	*Academic Writing Skill* Sentence variety *Rhetorical Mode* Opinion *Writing Task* Is disease prevention the responsibility of individuals and their families, or of the government? (essay)	*Life Skill* Managing minor illnesses
Analyzing a case study	Expressing solutions using *it*	*Academic Writing Skills* Developing ideas Parallel structure *Rhetorical Mode* Problem and solution *Writing Task* Write a report that provides both short- and long-term solutions to an environmental problem and takes the costs into consideration. Refer to a specific case study in your report. (report)	*Study Skill* Making a study plan

UNIT	WATCH AND LISTEN	READINGS	READING SKILLS	LANGUAGE DEVELOPMENT	
5 ARCHITECTURE *Academic Disciplines* Architecture / Urban Planning	Building a Green Home	1: We Need More Green Buildings (article) 2: Building Design: Form vs. Function (essay)	*Key Skill* Skimming a text *Additional Skills* Using your knowledge Understanding key vocabulary Summarizing Reading for details Understanding paraphrase Making inferences Synthesizing	Academic word families Architecture and planning vocabulary	
6 ENERGY *Academic Disciplines* Engineering / Physics	Wind Turbines	1: Alternative Energy (Web article) 2: Maintaining Our Vital Natural Resources (essay)	*Key Skill* Working out meaning from context *Additional Skills* Predicting content using visuals Understanding key vocabulary Using your knowledge Reading for main ideas Reading for details Making inferences Synthesizing	Energy collocations Formal and informal academic verbs	
7 ART AND DESIGN *Academic Disciplines* Design / Fine Art	A Culinary Art Canvas	1: All that Art Is (article) 2: Photography as Art (essay)	*Key Skill* Scanning to find information *Additional Skills* Understanding key vocabulary Predicting content using visuals Using your knowledge Reading for details Making inferences Understanding paraphrase Synthesizing	Paraphrasing Vocabulary for art and design	
8 AGING *Academic Disciplines* Economics / Sociology	Senior Exercise	1: The Social and Economic Impact of Aging (interview) 2: The Realities of a Young Society (essay)	*Key Skill* Using your knowledge to predict content *Additional Skills* Understanding key vocabulary Reading for main ideas Reading for details Working out meaning Making inferences Synthesizing	Academic collocations with prepositions	

CRITICAL THINKING	GRAMMAR FOR WRITING	WRITING	ON CAMPUS
Analyzing and evaluating ideas in persuasive writing	Register in academic writing	*Academic Writing Skills* Ordering information Prioritizing arguments *Rhetorical Mode* Persuasive *Writing Task* Which is more important when building or buying a new home: its location or its size? (essay)	*Life Skill* Resolving conflicts
Evaluating benefits and drawbacks Organizing ideas for an essay	Relative clauses	*Academic Writing Skills* Introducing advantages and disadvantages Coherence *Rhetorical Mode* Explanatory *Writing Task* Explain the advantages and disadvantages of three types of renewable energy and decide which would work best in your country. (essay)	*Communication Skill* Letters of reference
Analyzing and evaluating arguments	Substitution Ellipsis	*Academic Writing Skill* Arguments, counterarguments, and refutations *Rhetorical Mode* Argumentative *Writing Task* Fashion, cooking, and video games have all been likened to fine art. Choose *one* of these and discuss whether it should be considered fine art, comparable to painting or sculpture. (essay)	*Research Skill* Understanding common knowledge
Analyzing graphical data Evaluating advantages and disadvantages	Language of prediction Future real conditionals	*Academic Writing Skills* Numerical words and phrases Interpreting graphs and charts *Rhetorical Mode* Analysis *Writing Task* Describe population trends in Japan using data from a graph. Suggest the potential impact on the country if the 2050 projections are correct. (essay)	*Life Skill* The world of work

INTRODUCTION

***Prism* is a five-level paired skills series for beginner- to advanced-level students of North American English.** Its five Reading and Writing and five Listening and Speaking levels are designed to equip students with the language and skills to be successful both inside and outside of the college classroom.

***Prism* uses a fresh approach to Critical Thinking based on a full integration of Bloom's taxonomy to help students become well-rounded critical thinkers.** The productive half of each unit begins with Critical Thinking. This section gives students the skills and tools they need to plan and prepare for success in their Speaking or Writing Task. Learners develop lower- and higher-order thinking skills, ranging from demonstrating knowledge and understanding to in-depth evaluation and analysis of content. Margin labels in the Critical Thinking sections highlight exercises that develop Bloom's concepts.

***Prism* focuses on the most relevant and important language for students of academic English based on comprehensive research.** Key vocabulary is taken from the General Service List, the Academic Word List, and the Cambridge English Corpus. The grammar selected is also corpus-informed.

***Prism* goes beyond language and critical thinking skills to teach students how to be successful, engaged college students both inside and outside of the classroom.** On Campus spreads at the end of each unit introduce students to communication, study, presentation, and life skills that will help them transition to life in North American community college and university programs.

***Prism* combines print and digital solutions for the modern student and program.** Online workbooks give students additional graded language and skills practice. Video resources are available to students and teachers in the same platform. Presentation Plus gives teachers modern tools to enhance their students' learning environment in the classroom.

***Prism* provides assessment resources for the busy teacher.** Photocopiable unit quizzes and answer keys are included in the Teacher's Manual, with downloadable PDF and Word versions available at Cambridge.org/prism and in the Resource tab of the Cambridge Learning Management System. Writing rubrics for grading Writing Tasks in the Student's Book and on the Unit Writing Quizzes are included in the Teacher's Manual.

SERIES LEVELS

Level	Description	CEFR Levels
Prism Intro	Beginner	A1
Prism 1	Low Intermediate	A2
Prism 2	Intermediate	B1
Prism 3	High Intermediate	B2
Prism 4	Advanced	C1

UNIT OPENER

Each unit opens with a striking two-page photo related to the topic, a Learning Objectives box, and an Activate Your Knowledge activity.

PURPOSE

- To introduce and generate interest in the unit topic with an engaging visual
- To set the learning objectives for the unit
- To make connections between students' background knowledge and the unit topic/ theme

TEACHING SUGGESTIONS

PHOTO SPREAD

Lead an open class discussion on the connection between the unit opener photo and topic. Start off with questions like:

- *What is the first thing you notice in the photographs?*
- *What do you think of when you look at the photo?*
- *How is the photo connected to the unit title?*

ACTIVATE YOUR KNOWLEDGE

After students work in pairs to discuss the questions, have volunteers share with the class answers to questions that generated the most discussion.

You can also use the exercise to practice fluency. Instruct students to answer the questions as quickly as possible without worrying about creating grammatically correct sentences. Keep time and do not allow students more than 15–60 seconds per answer, depending on level and complexity of the question. You can then focus on accuracy when volunteers share their answers with the class.

WATCH AND LISTEN

Each unit includes a short authentic video from a respected news source that is related to the unit topic, along with exercises for students to do before, during, and after watching. The video can be played in the classroom or watched outside of class by students via the Cambridge LMS.

Note: A glossary defines above-level or specialized words that appear in the video and are essential for students to understand the main ideas so that teachers do not have to spend time pre-teaching or explaining this vocabulary while viewing.

PURPOSE

- To create a varied and dynamic learning experience
- To generate further interest in and discussion of the unit topic
- To build background knowledge and ideas on the topic
- To develop and practice key skills in prediction, comprehension, and discussion
- To personalize and give opinions on a topic

TEACHING SUGGESTIONS

PREPARING TO WATCH

Have students work in pairs to complete the Activating Your Knowledge exercise. Then have volunteers share their answers. Alternatively, students can complete this section on their own, and then compare answers with their partners.

For a livelier class discussion, look at the visuals from the Predicting Content Using Visuals exercise as a class and answer the questions together.

WHILE WATCHING

Watch the video twice, once while students listen for main ideas and once while they listen for key details. After each viewing, facilitate a discussion of students' answers and clarify any confusion. If some students still have trouble with comprehension, suggest that they watch the video again at home or during a computer lab session.

DISCUSSION

Have students work in pairs or small groups to answer the discussion questions. Have students compare their answers with another pair or group. Then have volunteers share their answers with the class. If possible, expand on their answers by making connections between their answers and the video content. For example: *That's an interesting perspective. How is it similar to what the speaker in the video mentioned? How is it different?*

For writing practice, have students write responses to the questions for homework.

READING

The first half of each unit focuses on the receptive skill of reading. Each unit includes two reading passages that provide different angles, viewpoints, and/or genres related to the unit topic.

READING 1

Reading 1 includes a reading passage on an academic topic. It provides information on the unit topic, and it gives students exposure to and practice with language and reading skills while helping them begin to generate ideas for their Writing Task.

PREPARING TO READ

PURPOSE

- To prepare students to understand the content of the reading
- To introduce, review, and/or practice key pre-reading skills
- To introduce and build key academic and topical vocabulary for the reading and for the unit Writing Task

TEACHING SUGGESTIONS

Encourage students to complete the pre-reading activities in this section in pairs or groups. This will promote a high level of engagement. Once students have completed the activities, check for understanding and offer any clarification.

Encourage or assign your students to keep a vocabulary notebook for new words. This should include new key vocabulary words, parts of speech, definitions (in the students' own words), and contextual sentences. To extend the vocabulary activity in this section, ask students to find synonyms, antonyms, or related terms for the vocabulary items they just practiced. These can then be added to their vocabulary notebooks.

Key vocabulary exercises can also be assigned ahead of time so that you can focus on the reading content and skills in class.

If time permits, have students scan Reading 1 for the key vocabulary just practiced in bold and read the sentences with each term. This will provide additional pre-reading scaffolding.

WHILE READING

PURPOSE

- To introduce, review, and/or practice key academic reading skills
- To practice reading comprehension and annotation skills
- To see and understand key vocabulary in a natural academic context
- To provide information and stimulate ideas on an academic topic
- To help students become more efficient readers

TEACHING SUGGESTIONS

Have students work in pairs or small groups to complete the activities. Students should always be prepared to support their answers from the text, so encourage them to annotate the text as they complete the activities. After students complete the activities, have volunteers share their answers with the class, along with support from the text. If necessary, facilitate clarification by referring back to the text yourself. Use guided questions to help with understanding. For example: *Take a moment to review the final sentences of Paragraph 2. What words discuss a problem?*

READING BETWEEN THE LINES

PURPOSE

- To introduce, expand on, and/or practice key reading skills related to students' ability to infer meaning, text type, purpose, audience, etc.
- To introduce, review, and/or practice key critical thinking skills applied to content from the reading passage

TEACHING SUGGESTIONS

Have students complete the activities in pairs or small groups and share their answers with the class. It is particularly important for students to be able to support their answers using the text at this point. Encourage students to work out any partial or wrong answers by asking a series of clear, guided questions like: *You thought the author meant ... What about this sentence in the reading? What information does it give us? Does this sentence change your mind about your answer?*"

After checking answers, survey students on what they found most challenging in the section. Then have students read the text again for homework, making additional annotations and notes on the challenging skills and content to be shared at the beginning of the next class or in an online forum.

DISCUSSION

PURPOSE

- To give students the opportunity to discuss and offer opinions about what they read
- To think critically about the content of the reading
- To further personalize the topic and issues in Reading 1

TEACHING SUGGESTIONS

Give students three to five minutes to discuss and jot down notes for their answers before discussing them in pairs or small groups. Monitor student groups, taking notes on common mistakes. Then, survey the students on their favorite questions and have groups volunteer to share these answers. You can provide oral or written feedback on common mistakes at the end of the section.

READING 2

Reading 2 is a reading passage on the unit topic from a different angle and often in a different format than Reading 1. It gives students additional exposure to and practice with language and reading skills while helping them generate and refine ideas for their Writing Task. It generally includes rhetorical elements that serve as a structured model for the Writing Task.

PREPARING TO READ

PURPOSE

- To prepare students to understand the content of the reading
- To introduce, review, and/or practice key pre-reading skills
- To introduce and build key academic and topical vocabulary for the reading and for the unit Writing Task

TEACHING SUGGESTIONS

As with Reading 1, encourage students to complete the activities in this section in pairs or small groups to promote a high level of engagement. Circulate among students at this time, taking notes of common areas of difficulty. Once students have completed the activities, check for understanding and offer clarification, paying particular attention to any problem areas you noted.

If you wish to extend the vocabulary activity in this section, elicit other word forms of the key vocabulary. Students can add these word forms to their vocabulary notebooks.

WHILE READING

PURPOSE

- To introduce, review, and/or practice key academic reading skills
- To practice reading comprehension and annotation skills
- To see and understand key vocabulary in a natural academic context
- To provide information and stimulate ideas on an academic topic
- To help students become more efficient readers
- To model aspects or elements of the Writing Task

TEACHING SUGGESTIONS

As with Reading 1, have students work in pairs or small groups to complete the activities. Encourage them to annotate the reading so that they are prepared to support their answers from the text. Elicit answers and explanations from the class. Remember to facilitate clarification by referring back to the text yourself, using clear, guided questions to help with understanding.

Alternatively, separate the class into multiple groups, and assign a paragraph or section of the reading to each groups. (Students should skim the rest of the passage not assigned to them.) Set a time limit for reading. Then do the exercises as a class, with each group responsible for answering and explaining the items that fall within their paragraph or section of the text.

READING BETWEEN THE LINES

PURPOSE

- To introduce, expand on, and/or practice key reading skills related to students' ability to infer meaning, text type, purpose, audience, etc.
- To introduce, review, and/or practice key critical thinking skills applied to content from the reading passage

TEACHING SUGGESTIONS

For Making Inferences activities, have students work in pairs to answer the questions. Instruct pairs to make notes in the margins about the clues from the text they use to answer the questions. Then have pairs meet up with other pairs to compare their clues. Have volunteers share their clues and answers with the class.

For other activity types, such as Recognizing Text Type or Distinguishing Fact and Opinion, have students work in pairs and then share their answers with the class as before. Then promote deeper engagement with guided questions like:

- *How is an essay different from a newspaper article?"*
- *What are common features of a* [text type]?"
- *What words in the sentence tell you that you are reading an opinion and not a fact?*
- *Can you say more about what x means?*

DISCUSSION

PURPOSE

- To personalize and expand on the ideas and content of Reading 2
- To practice synthesizing the content of the unit reading passages

Before students discuss the questions in this section the first time, introduce the key skill of synthesis. Start by defining synthesis (combining and analyzing ideas from multiple sources). Stress its importance in higher education: in college or graduate school, students will be asked to synthesize ideas from a wide range of sources, to think critically about them, to make connections among them, and to add their own ideas. Note: you may need to review this information periodically with your class.

Have students answer the questions in pairs or small groups, and then ask for volunteers to share their answers with the class. Facilitate the discussion, encouraging students to make connections between Reading 1 and Reading 2. If applicable, ask students to relate the content of the unit video to this section. This is also a good context in which to introduce the Writing Task at the beginning of the Critical Thinking section and to have students consider how the content of the reading passages relates to the prompt.

To extend this activity beyond discussion, write the connections students make on the board, and have students take notes. Students can then use their notes to write sentences or a paragraph(s) describing how the ideas in all the sources discussed are connected.

LANGUAGE DEVELOPMENT

Each unit includes the introduction and practice of academic language relevant to the unit topic and readings, and useful for the unit Writing Task. The focus of this section is on vocabulary and/or grammar.

PURPOSE
- To recycle and expand on vocabulary that appears in Reading 1 or Reading 2
- To focus and expand on grammar that appears in Reading 1 or Reading 2
- To expose students to additional corpus-informed, research-based language for the unit topic and level
- To practice language and structures that students can use in the Writing Task

TEACHING SUGGESTIONS

For grammar points, review the Language Box as a class and facilitate answers to any unclear sections. Alternatively, have students review it in pairs and allow time for questions. Then have students work in pairs to complete the accompanying activities. Review students' answers, allowing time for any clarification.

For vocabulary points, have students complete the exercises in pairs. Then, review answers and allow time for any clarification. To extend this activity, have students create sentences using each term and/or make a list of synonyms, antonyms, or related words and phrases for each term. Students should also add relevant language to their vocabulary notebooks. For homework, have students annotate the readings in the unit, underlining or highlighting any language covered in this section.

WRITING

The second half of each unit focuses on the productive skill of writing. It begins with the prompt for the Writing Task and systematically equips students with the grammar and skills to plan for, prepare, and execute the task successfully.

CRITICAL THINKING

PURPOSE
- To introduce the Writing Task.
- To notice and analyze features of Reading 2 related to the Writing Task
- To help generate, develop, and organize ideas for the Writing Task.
- To teach and practice the lower-order critical thinking skills of remembering, understanding, and applying knowledge through practical brainstorming and organizational activities

- To teach and practice the higher-order critical thinking skills of analyzing, evaluating, and creating in order to prepare students for success in the Writing Task and, more generally, in the college classroom

TEACHING SUGGESTIONS

Encourage students to work through this section collaboratively in pairs or small groups to promote a high level of engagement. Facilitate their learning and progress by circulating and checking in on students as they work through this section. If time permits, have groups exchange and evaluate one another's work.

Note: Students will often be directed back to this section to review, revise, and expand on their initial ideas and notes for the Writing Task.

GRAMMAR FOR WRITING

PURPOSE

- To introduce and practice grammar that is relevant to the Writing Task
- To introduce and practice grammar that often presents trouble for students at this level of academic writing

TEACHING SUGGESTIONS

Review any Skills boxes in this section as a class, allowing time to answer questions and clarify points of confusion. Then have students work on the activities in pairs or small groups, before eliciting answers as a class.

ACADEMIC WRITING SKILLS

PURPOSE

- To present and practice academic writing skills needed to be successful in college or graduate school
- To focus on specific language and skills relevant to the Writing Task

TEACHING SUGGESTIONS

Have students read any Skills boxes on their own. Check understanding by asking guided questions like:
- *What do you notice about the parallel structure examples?*
- *What are some other examples of parallel structure?*
- *How would you describe parallel structure based on the information and examples you just read?*

Provide clarification as necessary, offering and eliciting more examples. Have students find examples in the unit readings if possible.

Students can work in pairs to complete the exercises and then share their answers with the class. Alternatively, assign exercises for homework.

WRITING TASK

PURPOSE

- To work collaboratively in preparation for the Writing Task
- To revisit, revise, and expand on work done in the Critical Thinking section
- To provide an opportunity for students to synthesize the language, skills, and ideas presented and generated in the unit
- To help students plan, draft, revise, and edit their writing

TEACHING SUGGESTIONS

Depending on time and class level, students can complete the preparation activities for homework or in class. If conducted in class, have students work on their own to complete the Plan section. They can then share their plans in pairs. Give students time to revise their plans based on feedback from their partners.

Depending on time, students can write their first drafts at home or in class. Encourage students to refer to the Task Checklist before and after writing their first drafts. The checklist can also be used in a peer review of first drafts in class.

Note: At this stage, encourage students to focus on generating and organizing their ideas, and answering the prompt, rather than perfecting their grammar, which they will focus on during the Edit stage using the Language Checklist.

Even with a peer review, it is important to provide written feedback for your students, either on their first or second drafts. When doing so, look for common mistakes in student writing. Select at least one problem sentence or area from each student's draft, and conduct an edit correction exercise either as a class or in an online discussion forum. You can also select and review a well-written sentence from each draft to serve as models and to provide positive reinforcement.

ON CAMPUS

Each unit concludes with a unique spread that teaches students concepts and skills that go beyond traditional reading and writing academic skills.

PURPOSE

- To familiarize students with all aspects of the North American college experience
- To enable students to interact and participate successfully in the college classroom
- To prepare students to navigate typical North American college campus life

TEACHING SUGGESTIONS

PREPARING TO READ

Begin with an open discussion by asking students what they know about the topic. For example:

- *What is a study plan?*
- *Have you ever written an email to a teacher or professor?*
- *How do college students choose a major?*
- *What is a virtual classroom?*

You can also write the question on the board and assign as pair work, and have students share their answers with the class.

WHILE READING

Have students read the text and complete the accompanying activities. Have them read again and check their work. You can extend these activities by asking the following questions:

- *What did you find most interesting in this reading passage?*
- *What did you understand more clearly during the second reading?*
- *Who do you think wrote the text? Why?*

PRACTICE

Have students read any skills boxes silently. Give them two minutes to discuss the information with partners before they complete the exercises. Elicit from some volunteers how the exercises practice what they read in the text.

REAL-WORLD APPLICATION

Depending on time, you may want to assign the activities in this section as homework. Having students collaborate on these real-world tasks either inside or outside of the classroom simulates a common practice in college and graduate school. At the beginning of the week you can set up a schedule so that several student groups present their work during class throughout the week.

To extend this section, assign small related research projects, as applicable. For example, have students research and report on three websites with information on choosing a college major.

PRISM WRITING TASK RUBRIC

CATEGORY	CRITERIA	SCORE
Content and Development	• Writing completes the task and fully answers the prompt. • Content is meaningful and interesting. • Main points and ideas are fully developed with good support and logic.	

Organization	• Writing is well-organized and follows the conventions of academic writing:
	  • Paragraph – topic sentence, supporting details, concluding sentence
	  • Essay – introduction with thesis, body paragraphs, conclusion
	• Rhetorical mode(s) used is appropriate to the Writing Task.	

Coherence, Clarity, and Unity	• Sentences within a paragraph flow logically with appropriate transitions; paragraphs within an essay flow logically with appropriate transitions. • Sentences and ideas are clear and make sense to the reader. • All sentences in a paragraph relate to the topic sentence; all paragraphs in an essay relate to the thesis.	
Vocabulary	• Vocabulary, including expressions and transition language, is accurate, appropriate, and varied. • Writing shows mastery of unit key vocabulary and Language Development.	
Grammar and Writing Skills	• Grammar is accurate, appropriate, and varied. • Writing shows mastery of unit Grammar for Writing and Language Development. • Sentence types are varied and used appropriately. • Level of formality shows an understanding of audience and purpose. • Mechanics (capitalization, punctuation, indentation, and spelling) are strong. • Writing shows mastery of unit Academic Writing Skills.	

How well does the response meet the criteria?	Recommended Score
At least 90%	20
At least 75%	15
At least 60%	10
At least 50%	5
Less than 50%	0
Total Score Possible per Section	20
Total Score Possible	100

Feedback:

UNIT 1
ACTIVATE YOUR KNOWLEDGE

page 15
Answers will vary.

WATCH AND LISTEN

Exercise 1 page 16
Answers will vary.

Exercise 2 page 16
Answers will vary.

Exercise 3 page 16
1 DNS
2 F; Chinese consumers like flavors inspired by traditional Chinese food.
3 F; Many of these flavors are popular with Chinese consumers.
4 T
5 DNS

Exercise 4 page 17
1 American
2 Popular
3 sweet
4 competitive
5 unique

Exercise 5 page 17
1 b
2 a
3 c

Exercise 6 page 17
Answers will vary.

READING 1

Exercise 1 page 18
a fresh
b selling point
c discount
d ingredient
e perfectionist
f situated
g insist
h authenticity

Exercises 2–3 page 19
1 (use of informal language)
3 (opinion language, e.g., "so delicious," "worth every penny")
4 (current weekly grocery prices)

Exercise 4 page 20
Answers will vary. Possible answers:
1 He likes the delicious food, the fresh ingredients, and the authenticity of the cooking.
2 Its food is all locally sourced within 20 miles (32 kilometers) of the restaurant.
3 He asks if anyone has any idea why grocery prices have gone up recently.
4 She is upset because of the increased food prices; she doesn't know how she is supposed to feed her family.

Exercise 5 page 20
1 F; There is locally sourced food in the Minneapolis area and there are pockets of green all over the city.
2 T
3 DNS
4 T
5 DNS
6 T

Exercise 6 page 20
1 c
2 a
3 b

Exercise 7 page 20
Answers will vary. Possible answers:
1 Yes, because the delicious food at Moda results from having a perfectionist chef.
2 as a way to increase local awareness and business
3 TwinCitiesMom suggests that it is because of the recent awful weather (which might affect transportation or production costs).

Exercise 8 page 21
Answers will vary.

READING 2

Exercise 1 page 21
1 convenience
2 ensure
3 consumption
4 increase
5 relatively
6 specialty
7 influence
8 experiment

Exercises 2–3 page 22
Answers will vary.

Exercise 4 page 22
2 past
3 present
4 past
5 present
6 both

Exercise 5 page 22
Answers will vary. Possible answers:
1 all over the world
2 eat Asian food
3 foreign food
4 less common

Exercise 6 page 24
1 a
2 b

Exercise 7 page 24
Answers will vary.

LANGUAGE DEVELOPMENT

Exercise 1 page 24
1 b
2 a
3 f
4 c
5 h
6 d
7 g
8 e

Exercise 2 page 25
1 increase
2 continue
3 studying
4 confused
5 excluded
6 refused
7 exhausted
8 removed

Exercise 3 page 25
1 multinational
2 outlets
3 obesity
4 monopoly
5 poverty
6 diets
7 farms
8 supermarkets
9 consumption

CRITICAL THINKING

Exercise 1 page 26
Possible answers:
1 Until recently, pasta would have been made by people in their local area. Families would also have made the sauces to eat with the pasta at home.
2 Only pizza and pasta were available in the local town square.
3 Frozen or take-out meals, mass-produced dried pasta, and ready-made pasta sauces have become very popular. Fast food chains are seen as more convenient.
4 People worry about the destruction of local and national specialties. The Slow Food movement was started in Italy to encourage eating locally sourced food.
5 The popularity of foreign food, foreign chain restaurants, and convenient food are results of globalization, and this has changed the way Italians eat.

Exercises 2–3 pages 26–27
Answers will vary.

GRAMMAR FOR WRITING

Exercise 1 page 27
1 d
2 b
3 a
4 c

Exercise 2 page 28
2 a list of traditional dishes
3 television cooking programs
4 a noticeable increase in allergies and diabetes / diabetes and allergies
5 a variety of new fruits
6 the number of international chefs
7 the impact of different cultures
8 a great deal of time and preparation / preparation and time

Exercise 3 page 28

general past time	specific past time	present
before the war formerly historically in the past in recent years	around ten years ago in the 1990s in the eighteenth century	currently at the present time nowadays presently these days

Exercise 4 page 29
Answers will vary. Possible answers:
1 food from all over the world
2 foreign chains
3 Thai food in my country
4 cooking programs on television
5 Asian spices in the markets here
6 things they got from their farms

ACADEMIC WRITING SKILLS

Exercise 1 page 30
1 concluding
2 introductory
3 body
4 body
5 concluding

Exercise 2 page 31
1 F
2 Q
3 OK
4 G
5 OK
6 G
7 D

Exercise 3 page 31
1 b
2 c
3 a

WRITING TASK

Exercise 1 page 32
2, 1, 5, 3, 4

ON CAMPUS

Exercise 3 page 35
1 protein (yogurt, nuts, cheese, protein bars)
2 he sees and talks to people he knows
3 you can move around and reward yourself

UNIT 2
ACTIVATE YOUR KNOWLEDGE

page 37
Answers will vary.

WATCH AND LISTEN

Exercise 1 page 38
Answers will vary.

Exercise 2 page 38
Answers will vary.

Exercise 3 page 39
1 *Answers will vary.*
2 b

Exercise 4 page 39
1 student loan debt
2 $24,000
3 differences
4 three
5 bankruptcy
6 fine print

Exercise 5 page 39
Answers will vary.

Exercise 6 page 39
Answers will vary.

READING 1

Exercise 1 page 40
a pursue
b concrete
c launch
d oriented
e underrepresented
f evolve
g discipline
h gender gap

Exercise 2 page 41
2 discipline
3 gender gap
4 launch
5 oriented
6 underrepresented
7 concrete
8 evolve

Exercise 3 page 41
Answers will vary.

Exercise 4 page 43
1 both
2 engineering
3 business
4 engineering
5 both
6 both
7 engineering

Exercise 5 page 43
1 history, philosophy
2 take engineering courses in college
3 mechanical engineering
4 14%

Exercise 6 page 43

Answers will vary. Possible answers:

1 It's easier to find a job that way.
2 engineering: very specific and possibly not as transferable to different types of careers
   business: not as academic as other majors

Exercise 7 page 43

Answers will vary.

READING 2

Exercise 1 page 44

Answers will vary. Possible answers:

1 the trend toward more online learning
2 mechanical engineering
3 you can interact with the teacher and other students
4 you can earn it from your home
5 rechargeable batteries
6 communicate with people around the world
7 high standards of academic behavior are important
8 the cost of tuition

Exercise 2 page 44

Answers will vary.

Exercise 3 page 44

1 F
2 T
3 This depends on the course and the student's needs and goals.

Exercise 4 page 46

1 3
2 4
3 2
4 1

Exercise 5 page 46

1 face-to-face learning
2 distance learning
3 distance learning
4 both
5 distance learning
6 distance learning
7 both

Exercise 6 page 46

1 Because they consider distance learning to be directly linked to technological advances.
2 Because you do not generally meet your teachers face-to-face, you communicate with them in an online forum.
3 A face-to-face teacher can correct grammar or pronunciation in the moment. A distance-learning teacher writes or records feedback to send to the student later.
4 The author sees both the strengths and weaknesses of distance learning.

Exercise 7 page 47

Answers will vary.

LANGUAGE DEVELOPMENT

Exercise 1 page 47

1 assignment
2 semester
3 plagiarism
4 journal
5 teaching assistant
6 seminar
7 tutor
8 degree

Exercise 2 page 48

1 d
2 a
3 f
4 g
5 h
6 i
7 e
8 c
9 b

Exercise 3 page 48

1 alternative
2 significant
3 aspect
4 principles
5 motivation
6 specific
7 core
8 virtual

CRITICAL THINKING

Exercise 1 page 49

Answers will vary. Suggested answers:

distance learning:

– heavily dependent on technology (Internet)
– technology is the principal means of communication
– can happen at any time and in any location
– learners can learn at their own pace
– students must be highly motivated, well organized, and self-disciplined to do well
– teacher may seldom meet students; it can be hard for teachers to understand students' specific learning needs

face-to-face learning:

– students may only require a computer for the purpose of writing an essay
– takes place in real-time and in one location
– teacher and student have the opportunity to develop a
– personal relationship—the teacher becomes familiar with students' specific learning needs

similarities:
– teacher is responsible for helping students understand key information, decides how to present it to students
– teacher must create assignments for courses and help
– students know what resources they need
– teacher must provide feedback to students

Exercises 2–3 page 49
Answers will vary.

GRAMMAR FOR WRITING

Exercise 1 page 50
1 Conversely *or* In contrast
2 In the same way *or* Similarly
3 In contrast *or* Conversely
4 Similarly *or* In the same way

Exercise 2 page 50
Answers will vary.

Exercise 3 page 51
1 Academic courses focus on subjects like math, science, and literature, *while/whereas* vocational courses focus on practical skills. / *While/Whereas* vocational courses focus on practical skills, academic courses focus on subjects like math, science, and literature.
2 A university is a very large institution that offers undergraduate and graduate degrees, *while/whereas* a college is a smaller institution that typically offers only undergraduate degrees. / *While/Whereas* a university is a very large institution that offers undergraduate and graduate degrees, a college is a smaller institution that typically offers only undergraduate degrees.
3 Academic courses are theoretical, *while/whereas* vocational subjects are not. / *While/Whereas* academic courses are theoretical, vocational subjects are not.
4 More men tend to graduate with degrees in math or science, *while/whereas* more women tend to graduate with degrees in language or literature. / *While/Whereas* more men tend to graduate with degrees in math or science, more women tend to graduate with degrees in language or literature.

ACADEMIC WRITING SKILLS

Exercise 1 page 53
2 C *Possible answer*: ... college major. It is not as popular ...
3 R *Possible answer*: ... focuses on numbers, but language learning ...
4 C *Possible answer*: ... very popular; you can even ...
5 R *Possible answer*: academic subjects; other students ...
6 R *Possible answer*: ... charge tuition, but some are ...

Exercise 2 page 53
1 differences
2 both (but differences are more significant)
3 Reading 2

ON CAMPUS

Exercise 2 page 56

	Ricardo	Feride	Dylan
1 agrees with the discussion statement		✓	
2 disagrees with a classmate		✓	✓
3 uses sarcasm in his/her response			✓
4 states an opinion as a question		✓	
5 gives clear reasons for his/her opinion	✓	✓	
6 uses personal examples that support his/her argument	✓		
7 uses examples from class readings that support his/her argument		✓	
8 does not support his/her argument			✓
9 uses academic language	✓	✓	

Exercise 3 page 57
1 P
2 R
3 R
4 P
5 P
6 R

Exercise 4 page 57
Answers will vary.

UNIT 3
ACTIVATE YOUR KNOWLEDGE

page 59
Answers will vary. Possible answers to Question 1:
a cold: take some cold medicine, have some hot tea with honey, eat raw garlic
a headache: take some painkillers, drink lots of water
a cut on your hand: bandage it and raise it up, go to a hospital if it is serious
toothache: go to the dentist, take painkillers
obesity: eat less, exercise more
depression: talk to a therapist, take anti-depressants
stress: work less, exercise more

WATCH AND LISTEN

Exercise 1 page 60
Answers will vary.

Exercise 2 page 60
Answers will vary.

Exercise 3 page 61
a 5   b 1   c 4   d 3   e 6   f 2

Exercise 4 page 61
1 dogs, cats, trees, and dust
2 twelve
3 allergy shots or allergy drops
4 ten

Exercise 5 page 61
1

Exercise 6 page 61
Answers will vary.

READING 1

Exercise 1 page 62
1 b
2 b
3 a
4 a
5 b
6 b
7 a
8 a

Exercise 2 page 63
3

Exercise 4 page 63
1 F; Most health systems use conventional medicine.
2 T
3 T
4 DNS
5 F; Jessica Nogueira thinks that homeopathic remedies have much more than just a placebo effect.
6 T
7 DNS
8 T

Exercise 5 page 65
1 Piers Wehner
2 Jessica Nogueira
3 Piers Wehner
4 Jessica Nogueira
5 Jessica Nogueira
6 Jessica Nogueira
7 Piers Wehner
8 Piers Wehner

Exercise 6 page 65
Answers will vary. Possible answers:
1 Conventional medicine is very expensive because it needs a great deal of testing and the pharmaceutical companies want to make a large profit.
2 There is a great deal of evidence to show that if people believe they are being cured, they get better. This is called the placebo effect. People are less stressed if they believe that they are well.
3 People may be less worried if they have shared their medical problems and know that somebody is taking care of them. They may also be more motivated to take care of themselves.
4 Most mainstream doctors will say this, and this opinion is widespread and can be found everywhere.
5 Conventional medicine is based on science. Doctors also have to prove that they are not wasting money when using homeopathy.

Exercise 7 page 65
Answers will vary.

READING 2

Exercise 1 page 66
1 burden
2 treatment
3 regardless
4 safety net
5 consultation
6 contribution
7 labor

Exercise 2 page 66
Answers will vary.

Exercise 3 page 67
1 The article examines different kinds of public health care in different countries.

Exercise 4 page 68
1 *Answers will vary.*
2 *Possible answers*: public; private

Exercise 5 page 68
1 public
2 private
3 public
4 mixed
5 mixed

Exercise 6 page 68
synonyms of *people*: residents, citizens, workers, patients, individuals
synonyms of *money*: taxes, income, contribution, costs, funding, salaries, profit
related to *health care*: consultations, medicines, hospitals, medical services, health insurance, medical costs, preventative medicine, infectious diseases

Exercise 7 page 68
Answers will vary. Possible answers:
1 A person with a long-term illness might prefer free or public health care because of the continuing costs of treatment.
2 A person with a high income might prefer a private system because they could afford high-quality care.

Exercise 8 page 69
Answers will vary.

LANGUAGE DEVELOPMENT

Exercise 1 page 69
1 epidemic
2 underfunding
3 Drug dependency
4 sedentary lifestyle
5 preventable illness
6 patents

Exercise 2 page 70
1 adverse
2 professional
3 illegal
4 physical
5 complex
6 adequate
7 conventional
8 precise
9 medical

Exercise 3 page 70
1 illegal
2 professional
3 adequate
4 Conventional
5 complex
6 physical
7 adverse
8 medical
9 precise

CRITICAL THINKING

Exercise 1 page 71

support	oppose
no one is unable to afford health care; this type of system can help prevent the spread of diseases	free health care is sometimes only medium quality; private health care is often of higher quality; free health care for an entire country is complicated and expensive for a government; as life expectancy rises, it can result in an unsustainable financial burden for a government; citizens cannot choose their health-care options in a government-run system; there is less flexibility in public health care

Exercises 2–6 pages 71–72
Answers will vary.

Exercise 7 page 72
1 in favor
2 in favor
3 in favor
4 against
5 against
6 against
7 against
8 against
9 in favor

GRAMMAR FOR WRITING

Exercise 1 page 74
Letters show which article usage statement applies.
1 Ø (g); a (e)
2 Ø (f); Ø (h)
3 The (c)
4 The (d); the (b)
5 Ø (g or i)

Exercise 2 page 74

1 Conventional medicine is effective even though it may have unpleasant side effects.
2 Many people argue that homeopathy should be part of our health-care system. However, critics argue that it denies other people proven treatments.
3 Homeopathy is a popular choice for many in spite of the fact that there is no scientific evidence (that) it works.
4 Bathing in salt water is still commonly practiced in the twenty-first century, despite the fact that it is over 4,000 years old.

ACADEMIC WRITING SKILLS

Exercise 1 page 75
Answers will vary. Possible answers:
2 Although my country's health-care system is not perfect, it is better than many others.
3 This is the medication that I need to take for my illness.
4 All people in our society need access to affordable health care. It is their right.

ON CAMPUS

Exercise 2 page 78

1 Yes – they offer a stress reduction class and they mention stress reduction twice as a treatment.
2 stomachache or indigestion, trouble sleeping
3 a free bike helmet; biking is safer with a helmet, it provides protection in an accident
4 to make the patient more comfortable
5 *Possible answers:* they want to help you feel better, they are here to care for you

UNIT 4
ACTIVATE YOUR KNOWLEDGE

page 81
Answers will vary.

WATCH AND LISTEN

Exercise 1 page 82
Answers will vary.

Exercise 2 page 82
Answers will vary.

Exercise 3 pages 82–83
1 F; Only 1% of the fresh water is available for human use.
2 T
3 T

4 F; Water shortages are the result of increasing population, poor infrastructure, politics, poverty, or living in a dry part of the world.
5 F; The Aral Sea once covered more than 25,000 miles. It is now 10% of its original size.

Exercise 4 page 83
1 70%
2 distribution
3 population
4 infrastructure
5 common
6 space
7 drought

Exercise 5 page 83
Answers will vary.

Exercise 6 page 83
Answers will vary.

READING 1

Exercise 1 page 84
1 measure
2 identify
3 crucial
4 devastating
5 community
6 maintenance
7 reduction
8 criticize

Exercise 2 page 85
1 levee
2 dam
3 flood barrier
4 tsunami
5 hurricane
6 sandbagging

Exercise 3 page 86
1 "Controlling the Flow" is the best title because the interview is about ways to control the flow of water in a flood.
2 is not as good because it is too general and does not mention water or flooding.
3 is not as good because the interviewer says there are several ways, and people also have to help themselves in a flood situation.
4 is not as good because the text is not just about protecting houses.

Exercise 4 page 87
1 F; Dan Smith works for a government agency.
2 T
3 DNS
4 T
5 DNS
6 T

Exercise 5 page 87

1 risk reduction and risk analysis
2 risk reduction
3 earth-wall defenses, or levees
4 the case of a tsunami
5 the government agency
6 flood prevention solutions
7 construction of sea walls and bulkheads; redesign of power stations and subway tunnels; the Thames Barrier
8 expensive early warning systems

Exercise 6 page 88

Dan Smith would probably only agree with statement 5.

Exercise 7 page 88

1 and 2 *Answers will vary.*
3 *Possible answers:*
Bangladesh, China, India, Pakistan. Heavy monsoon rains and global warming means snow and ice on the Himalayas is melting into rivers and increasing the risk of flooding in these countries.

READING 2

Exercise 1 pages 88–89

1 disrupted
2 casualties
3 strategies
4 issue
5 monitor
6 rely on
7 infrastructure
8 policy

Exercise 2 page 89

Droughts are most common in countries that have little rain. These are predominantly found in sub-Saharan Africa. Australia also suffers badly, but as a richer country, it is better able to mitigate the problems arising from little or no rain. On the map, the areas with the highest temperatures (in red) and little rainfall are the ones most likely to suffer from drought: Africa and Australia.

Exercise 3 page 89

Answers will vary. Possible answers:
1 Drought kills animals and crops and causes starvation.
2 Bottles of drinking water can be brought into the drought area.
3 Drought monitoring, rainwater harvesting, and water recycling
4 Many long-term drought solutions are expensive and need technical knowledge that may not be available.

Exercise 4 page 91

a 6
b 5
c 1
d 4
e 3
f 2

Exercise 5 page 91

Possible answers:

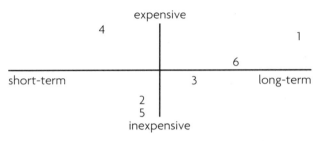

Exercise 6 page 91

1 b
2 b
3 a

Exercise 7 page 92

Answers will vary.

LANGUAGE DEVELOPMENT

Exercise 1 pages 92–93

2 Risk reduction
3 water-management system
4 government report
5 flood protection
6 Community-based projects

Exercise 2 page 93

1 natural
2 controlled
3 long-term
4 seasonal

Exercise 3 page 93

1 long-term projects
2 natural disasters
3 controlled floods
4 ambitious / large-scale projects
5 devastating / severe flood
6 extreme/prolonged drought
7 seasonal drought
8 terrible / major disaster

CRITICAL THINKING

Exercise 2 page 94
Suggested answer:

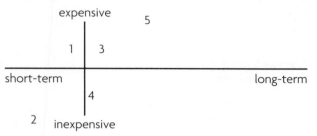

Exercise 3 page 95
Possible answers:
1 The cheaper ones would be easiest (government warning programs and shallow trench construction). The others might be too hard or expensive.
2 *Answers will vary.*
3 *Answers will vary*, but a logical answer might be the three cheapest options.

GRAMMAR FOR WRITING

Exercise 1 page 96
Answers will vary. Possible answers:
1 b
2 f
3 c
4 a
5 h
6 e
7 d
8 g

Exercise 2 page 96
Answers will vary. Possible answers:
1 using sandbags to stop water
2 on high ground
3 harvesting and storing rainwater
4 to get people to agree on a strategy
5 that they are expensive
6 crucial that people pay attention to it

ACADEMIC WRITING SKILLS

Exercise 1 page 97
a 3
b 1
c 2
d 4
e 5

Exercise 2 page 98
1 "talk to their friends and neighbors" – needs to be a noun phrase: "their friends and neighbors"
2 "they should establish desalination plants" – needs to be a gerund phrase: "establishing desalination plants"
3 "he analyzes risk" – should be a noun phrase: "risk analysis"
4 "the expense is surprising" – should be an adjective phrase: "surprisingly expensive"
5 "typhoons can also occur" – needs to be a noun with no verb: "typhoons"

ON CAMPUS

Exercise 2 page 100
1 The semester plan keeps track of important dates to help her plan her time. The weekly plan helps her prioritize tasks.
2 the weekly study plan
3 one is a calendar, the other is to-do lists

UNIT 5
ACTIVATE YOUR KNOWLEDGE

page 103
Answers will vary.

WATCH AND LISTEN

Exercise 1 page 104
Answers will vary.

Exercise 2 page 104
Answers will vary.

Exercise 3 pages 104–105
1 c
2 a
3 b

Exercise 4 page 105
1 1,000
2 1,200
3 0
4 68
5 71
6 300
7 115,000

Exercise 5 page 105
Statements 1 and 2 should be checked.

Exercise 6 page 105
Answers will vary.

READING 1

Exercise 1 page 106
Answers will vary.

Exercise 2 page 106
1 durable
2 compromise
3 efficiency
4 conservation
5 secondhand
6 sector
7 relevant

Exercise 3 page 107
d

Exercise 4 page 107
Answers will vary.

Exercise 5 page 107
a 2
b 3
c 1
d 5
e 4

Exercise 6 page 109
1 HH
2 HH
3 RC
4 N
5 HH
6 HH
7 RC
8 HH

Exercise 7 page 109
1 T
2 DNS
3 F; Environmentally friendly practices become less
  practical/too costly for large-volume construction.
4 DNS
5 F; Fossil fuels are non-renewable.
6 T
7 T

Exercise 8 page 109
Possible answers:
1 There is more awareness about global warming.
2 Students probably learn about the importance of
  natural resources and respect for the environment.
3 Lack of sunlight prevents panels from generating
  enough electricity.
4 Many people like to support environmentally friendly
  companies that seem "green," especially if it does not
  cost them any more money, because they feel like they
  are doing something good for the planet.

Exercise 9 page 109
Answers will vary.

READING 2

Exercise 1 page 110
1 b
2 a
3 a
4 a
5 b
6 a
7 b

Exercise 2 page 110
Answers will vary.

Exercise 3 page 110
The writer thinks that it is more important to design a
building that is functional.

Exercise 4 page 112
1 function
2 beauty
3 architects
4 reflect
5 moods/happiness
6 building
7 users
8 celebrated

Exercise 5 page 112
1 b
2 a
3 f
4 c
5 e
6 d

Exercise 6 page 113
1 They can create a more positive and inspired
  workforce. They allow the users of the building to
  function well. They can give a positive impression of
  the owner to other people.
2 It maximizes the number of planes that can fit in the
  airport terminal.
3 The buildings might reflect badly on them.
4 lighting, lack of or poor view from windows, the
  temperature inside the building (either too cold or too
  hot), decoration
5 If workers have been provided with a comfortable and
  pleasant working environment, they may feel more
  appreciated and want to work harder for the employer.

Exercise 7 page 113
Answers will vary.

LANGUAGE DEVELOPMENT

Exercise 1 page 114
1 environmental
2 environmentally
3 depression
4 depress
5 depressingly
6 responsible
7 responsibly
8 architecture
9 architectural
10 architecturally
11 efficiency
12 efficient

Exercise 2 page 114
1 environmental
2 Functionalism
3 efficiently
4 responsibly
5 depress
6 architecture
7 environment
8 responsible
9 depression
10 architectural

Exercise 3 page 115
1 structural engineer
2 Skyscrapers
3 urban sprawl
4 green belt
5 Suburban; outskirts
6 amenities

Exercise 4 page 115
Answers will vary. Possible answers:
1 ... to design environmentally friendly, cost-effective buildings.
2 ... consider their environmental impact.
3 ... it is important to protect the Earth.
4 ... it protects the countryside from urban sprawl.
5 ... sewers, municipal buildings, and sports facilities.
6 ... it increases people's dependence on cars.

CRITICAL THINKING

Exercise 1 page 116
Possible answers:
beauty advantages: They make our towns and cities more attractive; they reflect well on the community.
function advantages: Functional buildings are easy to use; they are efficient; they can save space; they can use fewer resources; they can save users time.

Exercises 2–4 page 116
Answers will vary.

GRAMMAR FOR WRITING

Exercise 1 page 117
1 fundamentally
2 Undoubtedly
3 critical
4 considerable investment
5 calculate
6 can be justified
7 there is no real benefit
8 has a positive impact on
9 and desire to work effectively
10 approximately
11 This supports the truthfulness of this notion.

Exercise 2 page 117
Possible answers:
1 provide the space and facilities that are needed
2 how much money an eco-friendly building will save in the long term
3 the well-being of the local community
4 there is plenty of sunlight
5 the people who use the buildings
6 constructing ugly buildings

ACADEMIC WRITING SKILLS

Exercise 1 page 118
1 In spite of this
2 this profession *or* it
3 This combination
4 it *or* this profession
5 For this reason

Exercise 2 page 119
1 a
2 a
3 a
4 b
5 a

Exercise 3 page 120
1 b
2 a
3 c
4 b
5 a
6 c

ON CAMPUS

Exercise 1 page 122
Answers will vary.

Exercise 2 page 122
1 F
2 T
3 F
4 T
5 F

UNIT 6
ACTIVATE YOUR KNOWLEDGE

page 125
1 solar power
2 Fossil fuels like coal and oil are formed underground from plant and animal remains millions of years ago. Renewable energy like solar power and hydropower is produced using the sun, wind, etc.
3 and 4 *Answers will vary.*

WATCH AND LISTEN

Exercise 1 page 126
Answers will vary.

Exercise 2 page 126
Answers will vary.

Exercise 3 page 127
1 T
2 F; The wind turbines in Sweetwater are responsible for producing 3% of the electricity for Texas.
3 F; Samuel Barr's windmill produces enough electricity to power everything in his home.
4 F; One criticism of wind turbines is that they are outside of the locations where the most power is needed.
5 T

Exercise 4 page 127
1 They have 3,200 turbines which generate 3% of the electricity.
2 He saved over $200 on his energy bill in the last month.
3 $9 billion was invested in new projects last year, making up 35% of all alternative energy investments.
4 The greatest demand is summer, and winds are not strong in summer, they have killed migratory birds, and many find them unattractive.

Exercise 5 page 127
Answers will vary.

Exercise 6 page 127
Answers will vary.

READING 1

Exercise 1 page 128
1 wind power
2 geothermal energy
3 solar power
4 hydropower

Exercise 2 page 128
a initial
b generate
c aquatic
d offshore
e universal
f utilize
g inexhaustible

Exercise 3 page 130
c "An Overview of Renewable Energy Production"

Exercise 4 page 130
1 solar
2 biomass
3 geothermal
4 hydropower
5 solar
6 geothermal

Exercise 5 page 130
1 hydropower
2 wind
3 biomass
4 solar
5 geothermal
6 hydropower
7 biomass

Exercise 6 page 131
1 solar: related to the sun
2 fragile: easily broken, damaged or harmed
3 store: to put or keep things for use in the future
4 geothermal: involving or produced by the heat that is inside the Earth
5 wildlife: animals that live independently of people, in natural conditions
6 bury: to put something into the ground
7 bounded by: surrounded or limited by

Exercise 7 page 131
Answers will vary.

READING 2

Exercise 1 page 132
1 urgent
2 alarming
3 adopt
4 address
5 diminish
6 vital
7 resistant
8 instigated

Exercise 2 page 132
Answers will vary. Possible answers:
2 droughts; problems with growing crops; the death of livestock and other animals
3 less food and fewer habitats for animals; flooding due to excess water run-off
4 food prices would rise and there could be riots, starvation, and death
5 prices of metals would rise sharply; consumer goods would be more expensive

Exercise 3 page 133
Answers will vary. Possible answers:
2 Build water storage facilities (dams, irrigation channels, etc.)
3 Protect forests; create national parks; plant new trees; build dams to stop serious flooding
4 Reduce food waste through education; encourage people to eat produce that needs less land; enforce fishing quotas
5 Find new sources of metal; ensure that metal is recycled from old items

Exercise 4 page 133
Answers will vary. Possible answers:
Reduce means to consume and use less. We can reduce our use of electricity, gas, oil, and chemicals for example. Reuse means to use things again, for example, plastic bags from the supermarket or plastic containers. Recycle means to collect and treat garbage in order to produce useful materials. Paper, glass, and some metals and plastics can be recycled.

Exercise 6 page 133
1 No, it isn't.
2 Some energy sources may not be available to all people in certain places because of environmental limitations or cost.
3 It is crucial that we "go green" for the future of the planet by reducing, reusing, and recycling.

Exercise 7 page 133
2 motorized
3 medical; food-storage
4 metals
5 fossil fuels
6 solar; geothermal
7 the planet

Exercise 8 page 135
Possible answers:
1 They are unlikely to change their habits unless it affects them financially.
2 It produces a lot of carbon emissions from fossil fuels.
3 It might contain dangerous bacterial, viral, or medicinal substances.
4 They might not want to make changes that increase their production costs even if they help the environment.

Exercises 9 page 135
Answers will vary.

LANGUAGE DEVELOPMENT

Exercise 1 page 135
1 fuel
2 energy
3 pollution
4 source
5 production
6 problem

Exercise 2 page 136
1 nuclear
2 health/medical
3 source
4 fossil
5 Alternative/Renewable
6 water

Exercise 3 page 136
1 d
2 h
3 g
4 f
5 c
6 b
7 a
8 e

Exercise 4 page 136
1 diminish
2 deliver
3 contested
4 consult
5 instigate
6 utilizes
7 omit
8 secure

CRITICAL THINKING

Exercises 1–4 pages 137–138
Answers will vary.

GRAMMAR FOR WRITING

Exercise 1 page 139
1 who (Enrico Fermi)
2 whose (people)
3 where (cabinet)
4 when (at night)
5 which (ethanol)

Exercise 2 page 140
1 that (no commas required)
2 Solar power, **which** is a form of renewable energy, is very popular in southern Spain.
3 that (no commas required)
4 that (no commas required)
5 who (no commas required)
6 Al Gore, **who** is a key supporter of alternative energy, won the Nobel Prize in 2007.

ACADEMIC WRITING SKILLS

Exercise 1 page 140
Answers will vary. Possible answers:
2 The most serious disadvantage of biomass is that it produces greenhouse gases.
3 Another potential disadvantage of biomass is that large areas of land are needed.
4 The most obvious advantage of hydropower is that energy can be stored and used when it is needed.
5 An apparent disadvantage of geothermal energy is that it is only available in certain places.

Exercise 2 page 141
1 For example,
2 however,
3 they
4 this
5 In the same way
6 they

Exercise 3 page 141
Answers will vary. Example paragraph:
Turbines and hydropower plants both change the landscape of an area. Even though some people think they alter the natural landscape in an unattractive way, others think that they are important sources of alternative energy. It is important to use alternative energy sources so that we are less dependent on fossil fuels, which have been linked to global warming. There is resistance to this idea, however. Some people are more concerned about using fossil fuels than other people are. Also, some think it is more important save money than to reduce global warming, and alternative energy production facilities can be expensive to construct.

ON CAMPUS

Exercise 1 page 144
Answers will vary.

Exercise 2 page 144

1 She gave the professor enough time to respond.	✓
2 She used the professor's first name.	✓
3 She said where she planned to study.	✓
4 She didn't say what she planned to study.	
5 She didn't say why she chose that college.	
6 She reminded the professor which course she took with him.	✓
7 She gave additional details about her coursework.	✓
8 She didn't send additional personal information or documents.	
9 She wrote in a professional tone throughout.	✓
10 She gave a due date for the letter.	✓

UNIT 7
ACTIVATE YOUR KNOWLEDGE

page 147
Answers will vary.

WATCH AND LISTEN

Exercise 1 page 148
Answers will vary.

Exercise 2 page 148
Answers will vary.

Exercise 3 page 149
a 6
b 3
c 4
d 2
e 5
f 1

Exercise 4 page 149
1 She has more than 46,000 followers on Tumblr.
2 Her favorite is the stall right outside her door.
3 She uses radishes to make a daisy.
4 Pieces made in early morning or later afternoon have the right sunlight.

Exercise 5 page 149
Answers will vary.

Exercise 6 page 149
Answers will vary.

READING 1

Exercise 1 page 150
1 conceptual
2 aesthetic
3 contemporary
4 distinction
5 established
6 significance
7 notion

Exercise 2 page 151
1 b
2 d
3 a
4 c

Exercise 3 page 151
a 1
b 4
c 3
d 2

Exercise 4 page 153
1 T
2 F; Metalworking is an example of applied art.
3 T
4 DNS
5 DNS
6 F; "Art for art's sake" refers to fine art.
7 DNS
8 F; Damian Hirst's assistants produce his art, although the ideas are his own.

Exercise 5 page 153
1 Hirst
2 Warhol
3 Duchamp
4 Banksy
5 Hirst
6 Wright

Exercise 6 page 153
Answers will vary.

READING 2

Exercise 1 page 154
Answers will vary.

Exercise 2 page 154
1 a
2 b
3 a
4 b
5 a
6 a
7 b
8 a

Exercise 3 page 154
1 paragraph 1
2 paragraph 3
3 paragraph 2
4 paragraph 4

Exercise 4 page 156
1 b
2 a
3 a

Exercise 5 page 156
1 d
2 c
3 a
4 e
5 b

Exercise 6 page 157
1 c
2 d
3 a
4 e
5 b

Exercise 7 page 157
Answers will vary.

LANGUAGE DEVELOPMENT

Exercise 1 page 158
Answers will vary. Possible answers:
1 insisted
2 suggested
3 maintained
4 denied (note that *denied* means *said that you had not done something*, so it is used with a positive verb)

Exercise 2 page 159
Possible answers:
1 Horace pointed out that a picture is like a work of literature without words.
2 Henri Matisse felt that being creative required overcoming cowardice.
3 Leonardo da Vinci stated that a painter uses his or her mind and hands to paint unlimited subjects.

Exercise 3 page 159
1 monumental
2 moving
3 decorative
4 lifelike
5 avant-garde
6 abstract
7 figurative
8 expressive

CRITICAL THINKING

Exercise 1 page 160
Paragraph 2:
Argument: Photography is not on the same artistic level as other fine art.
Argument against: It is true that that photography can be appreciated like other forms of art, but it cannot be considered the same.
Why other side is wrong: Photographers have to call themselves *artists* (instead of *photographers*) in order to sell their work for a lot of money.
Paragraph 3:
Argument: The beauty of photography does not come from the photographer in the same way that the beauty of art comes from an artist.
Argument against: We can appreciate a beautiful photograph.
Why other side is wrong: Beauty comes from the time and place that the photograph was taken, and is not the result of a photographer's creativity.

Exercise 2 page 161
1 challenge
2 support
3 support
4 challenge
5 challenge
6 support

Exercise 3 page 161
Answers will vary.

GRAMMAR FOR WRITING

Exercise 1 page 162
the two-seater roadster; the car; the E-type; the machine; the car; it

Exercise 2 page 162
The Scream is the popular name given to each of four paintings ~~of The Scream~~ by the artist Edvard Munch who painted ~~The Scream~~ (them) between 1893 and 1910. The National Gallery in Oslo holds one painting ~~of The Scream~~, the Munch Museum holds two more paintings ~~of The Scream~~, and the fourth version ~~of The Scream~~ sold for $119 million at Sotheby's on May 2, 2012. To explain the picture ~~of The Scream~~, the artist Edvard Munch wrote in his diary, "One evening I felt tired and ill. I stopped and looked out over the sea—the sun was setting, and the clouds were turning blood red. I sensed a scream passing through nature; it seemed to me that I heard the scream."

ACADEMIC WRITING SKILLS

Exercise 1 page 163
1 a (A statistic is an effective way to support a thesis.)
2 b (Choice a is less persuasive since not all readers will agree with the logic of the statement.)
3 b (Choice b uses facts to support the argument.)

Exercise 2 page 164
Answers will vary. Possible answers:
1 art is important since it encourages creativity and self-expression, which are important skills.
2 everyone should be able to enjoy art, not just the rich.
3 argue that public art is expensive and does not contribute to the community.

Exercise 3 page 164
Answers will vary.

ON CAMPUS

Exercise 1 page 166
Answers will vary.

Exercise 2 page 166
1 CK
2 C
3 CK
4 CK
5 C
6 C

Exercise 2 pages 166–167
Students should highlight these sentences:
In 2002, approximately 25% of Americans visited art museums and galleries, but now only 20% are visiting. One survey done by the National Endowment for the Arts shows that lack of time is the biggest reason that people don't participate in the arts, followed by cost.

UNIT 8
ACTIVATE YOUR KNOWLEDGE

page 169
Answers will vary.

WATCH AND LISTEN

Exercise 1 page 170
Answers will vary.

Exercise 2 page 170
Answers will vary.

Exercise 3 page 171
Sentence 2

Exercise 4 page 171
Answers will vary. Possible answers:
1 Its goal is to make seniors feel more powerful.
2 There are over 2 million senior citizens who visit the emergency room every year.
3 She can do a mile on the treadmill now.

Exercise 5 page 171
Answers will vary.

Exercise 6 page 171
Answers will vary.

READING 1

Exercise 1 page 172
a capacity
b demographic
c leisure
d voluntary
e adapt
f undertake

Exercise 2 page 172
Answers will vary.

Exercise 3–4 page 173
Answers will vary. Possible answers:
1 Yes, it has.
2 People are living longer in most regions.
3 Old people may be unable to care for themselves for health reasons.
4 If old people are retired and not paying taxes but still need healthcare, this could put a strain on social systems.
5 The benefits could be that less money is needed for education. Older people may have saved money to spend on themselves and their families and may give time to voluntary organizations, or be able to help care for younger family members.

Exercise 5 page 174
1 DNS
2 T
3 F; In many countries, an increasing number of older people are living by themselves, often without any relatives living nearby.
4 T
5 F; Supermarkets have responded by providing more home-delivery services, and there has been a significant growth in companies providing services that would have traditionally been done by family members.
6 F; In countries where the percentage of children and young people is lower, there are lower costs in the education system.
7 DNS
8 T

Exercise 6 page 174
1 take care of
2 social activities
3 private nursing care
4 economic impact
5 savings, leisure time
6 voluntary

Exercise 7 page 175
Possible answers:
1 Scientific advances, healthier diets, and less poverty in many places increase life expectancy.
2 People are more mobile nowadays; they often have to move away from their families to find jobs.
3 People are busier these days, and maybe lazier too!
4 They may have been saving for a long time. They do not have to spend so much money on their children, who are now adults.
5 Older people can study at their own pace. They can also study subjects they are interested in rather than ones they need for a job.

Exercise 8 page 175
Answers will vary.

READING 2

Exercise 1 page 175
Answers will vary.

Exercise 2 page 176
1 a
2 b
3 a
4 b
5 c
6 a
7 c

Exercise 3 page 176
Having a younger overall population creates several challenges for Saudi Arabia, including education costs, unemployment, and housing shortages. However, health care and pension costs are lower.

Exercise 4 page 178
1 young
2 16
3 36
4 26; Japan
5 education
6 sectors
7 expansion

Exercise 5 page 178
1 if you consider the facts carefully
2 spending
3 very specific problems that require specific solutions
4 as a result or effect of something

Exercise 6 page 178
Answers will vary.

LANGUAGE DEVELOPMENT

Exercise 1 page 179
1 in
2 of
3 on
4 up
5 with
6 in
7 on
8 in

Exercise 2 page 179
1 rely on
2 In contrast
3 range of
4 focus on
5 In brief
6 in theory
7 identify with
8 sum up

CRITICAL THINKING

Exercise 1 page 180
1 2016
2 28,160,273
3 under 65
4 no

Exercise 2 page 180
1 The data is from January 2012.
2 around 127 million people
3 over 65
4 Saudi Arabia's shows a much larger population of young people. People in Japan are not having as many children as people in Saudi Arabia.

Exercise 3 page 181
Answers will vary.

Exercise 4 page 181
1 Increased health care costs
2 youth unemployment
3 Higher taxes
4 higher pension costs
5 declining birthrate
6 increased immigration

Exercise 5 page 181
Answers will vary.

GRAMMAR FOR WRITING

Exercise 1 page 182
1 b
2 a
3 e
4 d
5 g
6 c
7 f

Exercise 2 page 182
Answers will vary. Possible answers:
1 The population is likely to increase in the future.
2 Oil prices may come down this year.
3 Unemployment is predicted to remain at the same level in the coming months.
4 The cost of living is set to rise over the decade.
5 There is expected to be more competition for spots in colleges and universities in the future. / More competition for spots in colleges and universities is expected in the future.
6 There is unlikely to be a reduction in the number of schools. / A reduction in the number of schools is unlikely.
7 Salaries are projected to rise because of access to better training and education.

Exercise 3 page 183

1 will face, ages
2 continues, will live
3 will move in, agrees
4 does not, will face

Exercise 4 page 183

Answers will vary. Possible answers:

1 If a country has an aging population, the result will be fewer children.
2 Fewer people will pay income taxes if more people retire.
3 Provided that a country provides better education, its young people will find good jobs in other countries.
4 As long as the population continues to get younger, the government should prioritize public funds for the young over the aging.

ACADEMIC WRITING SKILLS

Exercise 1 page 184

1 majority
2 minority
3 times
4 proportion
5 double
6 triple
7 half
8 quarter

Exercise 2 page 185

1 No, it is not necessary to relate something so specific from the chart.
2 No, this is an opinion and is not data from the graph.
3 Yes, this is an observable trend.
4 Yes, this describes the data on the chart.
5 Yes, this is a prediction relevant to the data on the chart.

WRITING TASK

Exercise 1 page 186

2, 4, 3, 6, 5, 1

Exercise 2 page 185

Answers will vary. Possible answer:
The graph shows the proportion of three age ranges of the population of Japan since 1950 and predicts what those ranges will be through the year 2050.

ON CAMPUS

Exercise 1 page 188

Answers will vary.

Exercise 2 page 188

on-campus jobs:
for full-time students
internships:
related to major
paid or unpaid work
sometimes required for program
for full-time students
co-op programs:
related to major
work and study alternate quarters
for full-time students

Exercise 3 page 188

Answers will vary. Possible answers:

1 Students must also focus on their studies, not just work.
2 Many students need to get experience in their field before they graduate.
3 Advantages of an internship are practical knowledge (work experience) and college credits. Advantages of a co-op program are that students focus on either working or studying at one time, and all co-op programs have paid positions.

UNIT 1

▶ Chinese Flavors for American Snacks

Reporter: This Beijing supermarket's filled with brands that might look familiar but flavors that definitely aren't. Blueberry-flavored potato chips, strawberry and milk-flavored Cheetos? What about aloe juice from Minute Maid? Every major U.S. food label, it seems, is trying to bite into China's 186-billion-dollar fast-food and processed-food industries by creating new products designed just for Chinese taste buds. Tropicana cantaloupe juice, orange-flavored Chips Ahoy cookies, and Chinese herbal medicine Wrigley's Gum. But it's Frito-Lay potato chips that really push the boundaries. Early taste tests revealed that Chinese people didn't like popular American flavors like sour cream and onion. So product researchers came up with new flavors inspired by traditional Chinese food. From Sichuan spicy to sweet and sour tomato, all the way to the sugary end of the spectrum with cucumber flavor, lychee, and mango.

Harry Hui: The market is extremely competitive, so there are many new products that are being launched regularly onto the marketplace.

Reporter: Popular American chains are also getting in on the idea. McDonald's has purple taro pie. Starbucks offers coffee drinks with jelly cubes on the bottom. And KFC's got spicy squid on a stick.

These products may seem wacky in the U.S., but there's serious pressure to be the object of Chinese cravings.

Shaun Rein: China is going to become the second largest, if not largest, consumer market in the world in the next five years. So if American companies don't figure out how to get it right in China, they're going to be missing out on what should be their major generator for growth.

Reporter: Even the toothpaste companies can't afford to ignore the flavor game. From lotus flower Crest to salty Colgate. Every corner of the grocery store is trying to tempt China's curious consumers.

UNIT 2

▶ College Debt and Bankruptcy

Velicia Cooks: What's that one again?

Reporter: Velicia Cooks always believed a college degree would mean a better future, but at 30, faced with $80,000 in student loan debt, the future is hard to think about.

Velicia Cooks: I actually, currently, make almost exactly what I made before I had my degree.

Reporter: Today two-thirds of all students graduate in debt. The average debt is $24,000, but thousands begin their adult lives more than $100,000 in debt.

Woman: Some people say it's like graduating when you already have a mortgage, but you don't have a house.

Reporter: But the real shock comes with the repayment terms. Like many students, Cooks signed up for two kinds of loans; one federal and one private, but at the time she admits she didn't understand the distinction. Today, her $40,000 federal loan offers flexible options. Cooks pays $160 a month, but the private loan of the same amount came with very expensive, non-negotiable terms costing her $800 a month. Add the interest, Cooks will be paying $100,000—almost three times the original loan.

Woman: Private student loans are much more like a credit card or a sub-prime mortgage. They tend to have variable rates and they come with almost no consumer protections.

Reporter: For Cooks, keeping up with payments during a complicated pregnancy became too much to handle.

Velicia Cooks: To get those harassing phone calls, and it made me feel like I was a deadbeat.

Reporter: Cooks was advised to file for bankruptcy. Bad idea. Under the bankruptcy law, student loans cannot be discharged, unlike a mortgage, credit card, or even gambling debt.

That education debt stays with you for life.

Velicia Cooks: It stays with you for life. I prided myself as being financially responsible.

Reporter: Cooks testified before the House Judiciary Committee to help repeal the law which prevents people from discharging private student loan debt.

Velicia Cooks: It was irresponsible on my part, wholeheartedly, for not reading the fine print. Come get me!

Reporter: For many like Cooks, that fine print will cast a big shadow for a long time.

UNIT 3

▶ A New Way to Handle Allergies

Anchor: If you forget to take your meds, doctors have come up with an easy and convenient way to make sure you get your daily dose. Marlie Hall reports.

Marlie Hall (Reporter): Derek Lacarrubba is brushing his teeth and treating his allergies at the same time.

Derek Lacarrubba: Like there's nothing about it that seems any different than an ordinary toothpaste.

Marlie Hall: The 31-year-old is allergic to dogs, cats, trees, and dust. He's one of 12 patients testing the toothpaste called Allerdent at Weill Cornell Medical College.

Dr. William Reisacher: And we have our extracts.

Marlie Hall: The toothpaste is custom-made for patients and contains extracts of what they're allergic to.

Dr. William Reisacher: So if you can contact those extracts with the lining of the mouth, then you can desensitize a patient to those allergens and essentially cure them of their allergies.

Marlie Hall: Dr. William Reisacher developed the toothpaste. He's studying whether Allerdent is more effective than weekly allergy shots or daily allergy drops.

Dr. William Reisacher: The problem is when you send a treatment home, then people forget to do it, and also it's difficult for small children to keep a liquid under their tongue for two minutes.

Marlie Hall: The toothpaste can treat up to ten different allergies at one time. There can be side effects including itching and tingling in the mouth. Lacarrubba says Allerdent has helped with his stuffy nose, and his snoring and sleep are better.

Derek Lacarrubba: I can breathe through my nose on almost all mornings.

Marlie Hall: And he can even take his dog for a walk outside and enjoy it. Marlie Hall, CBS News, New York.

UNIT 4

▶ Population and Water

Narrator: We call our Earth "the blue planet" because about 70% of the Earth's surface is covered in water. But most of that is in the oceans and seas. Just 2.5% is fresh water, and only 1% of that is available for human use. The rest is locked up in mountain passes and the Earth's polar ice caps. But there's another fact we need to understand about water.

Brian Richter: Well, there's no more water on the planet than there was when life first appeared on Earth. It changes its distribution, there's more water in different parts of the world than there were hundreds or thousands of years ago, but it's still exactly the same amount of water that's been here always.

Narrator: We use over half of all the available fresh water in the world to serve our needs: to transform deserts into fields, to produce energy from rivers, and to build cities in some of the driest regions on the planet. But despite our creativity, there are many who have difficulty getting enough of this basic resource.

Brian Richter: More than a billion people on the planet already lack access to safe, clean drinking water. And we know things are going to get more difficult as the population continues to grow. Within the next 20 years, as much as half of the world's population will live in areas of water stress.

Narrator: Many water shortages are the result of poor infrastructure, politics, poverty, or simply living in a dry part of the world. But more and more, they are due to increasing populations. Mexico City, for example, benefits from heavy annual rainfall. But its water system is stressed from supplying water to its 20 million inhabitants. The issue is the combination of leaks in the system and the fact that backup reservoirs are running dry.

In Mexico City, shops that sell water for people's daily needs are becoming more and more common. But the water we use at home is only a small percentage of the total amount of water we consume. That's because of the huge amounts used by farms and factories.

Brian Richter: We may know where the water out of our tap comes from, but we very seldom know where the water that went into our can of cola or into the shirt that we're wearing on our back, where those goods were produced and how much water it required, and what the consequences were for the natural systems in those areas and for the local communities that are dependent upon that same water.

So for example, the cup of coffee that you may have in the morning requires on the order of 120 liters just to produce the coffee and bring it to your table. A can of beer 150 liters, a hamburger 8,000 liters of water, to produce enough water to grow the cotton in my shirt is 3,000 liters as well.

Narrator: The influence of humans on the world's fresh water systems is so significant that it can be seen from space. The Aral Sea, the fresh water lake in central Asia, once covered more than 25,000 square miles. But in the last 40 years, it has lost 90% of its water, with most of it going to support cotton farms. Lake Chad, on the southern side of the Sahara Desert, is now one tenth of its normal size due to drought and overuse. Yet, 30 million people still depend on it.

UNIT 5

▶ Building a Green Home

Dan Sharp: There's a lot of compost here.

Ben Tracy (Reporter): Dan Sharp decided it was time to do his part to save the planet.

Dan Sharp: A lot of things we were consuming, ways that we were living that we didn't necessarily need to be doing.

Ben Tracy: For the past five years, he's been systematically turning his century-old yellow house in Pasadena green. Dan installed solar panels on the roof, added solar tube-lighting inside, and replaced the AC with a giant house fan.

Dan Sharp: It's a little louder than a normal air conditioner, but it, you know, costs much, much less to operate.

Ben Tracy: Dan's wife, Maya, wasn't so sure about all these eco upgrades until she saw their annual electric bill.

Maya Sharp: Before it would be $1,000, $1,200 a year and now it's zero.

Ben Tracy: That type of savings has homeowners jumping on the green bandwagon. A recent survey found that 68% of those polled took steps last year to make their homes more energy efficient. Yet 71% of them said their number one reason was to save money, not necessarily the environment. Home builders struggling to find buyers in a tough market are taking note.

Man 1: This is really nice.

Ben Tracy: They're rolling out smaller, greener models, hoping to attract first-time homebuyers. What are you looking for in this sort of market?

Man 1: Cheap.

Ben Tracy: Comstock Homes is building the country's largest solar-powered community just outside Los Angeles. The sun power generated could save homeowners as much as $300 on their monthly utility bills. They think it will also spike home sales.

Man 2: By adding the solar to it, it allows us to absorb probably twice as fast the number of buyers that we normally would.

Ben Tracy: Meanwhile, Greenstreet Development, a housing startup in Phoenix, is selling green homes for as low as $115,000. They keep costs down by buying foreclosed properties and renovating them with energy-saving features.

Yet one of the biggest selling points of these homes is not the savings inside, it's the savings a couple of blocks away. All of the homes are within a quarter mile of the city's new light-rail line, cutting down on commuting time and cost.

Still, there's a limit on how much consumers will spend to go green.

Man 3: They're only willing to pay about 2% more than the cost of a house would normally be in order to get it green, that's a difficult balance for a builder to achieve.

Dan Sharp: In the long term, you will save money, you will definitely recoup your initial investment.

Ben Tracy: And that means Dan Sharp is seeing less of his hard-earned money washed away. Ben Tracy, CBS News, Los Angeles.

UNIT 6

▶ Wind Turbines

Daniel Sieberg (Reporter): Jerry Tuttle is a new breed of cowboy.

Jerry Tuttle: The whole desk job thing is just not for me.

Daniel Sieberg: His herd is hundreds of giant wind turbines. I climbed with Tuttle, nearly 300 feet in the air, so we could show off his penthouse office. This is a pretty amazing workplace.

Jerry Tuttle: Well look at it, look at it, I mean that is, it is what it is, it's amazing.

Daniel Sieberg: As a turbine technician, Tuttle keeps things humming at this massive farm in Sweetwater, Texas. With 3,200 turbines, wind generates 3% of the electricity in Texas, more than any other state.

Jerry Tuttle: It's nice to know that we are, we are putting renewable energy down, and with zero pollution.

Daniel Sieberg: Companies are doing it big in Texas, but homeowners can do it small, in their own backyards.

Samuel Barr: Well, I don't screw up the environment, I save a few bucks, and it's not a bad deal.

Daniel Sieberg: In Oneida, New York, Samuel Barr's personal windmill powers everything from his cappuccino machine to his kids' computer. It cost $58,000, but the state picked up half. Last month alone, he saved over $200 and his meter sometimes even spins backwards.

Samuel Barr: When we first put it up, I'd spend hours looking at this meter.

Daniel Sieberg: In disbelief?

Samuel Barr: Yeah, in disbelief, yeah.

Daniel Sieberg: The wind rush is on. $9 billion was invested in new wind projects last year alone—35% of alternative energy investments. But critics say it's mostly hot air.

Woman: You're building, typically building the projects way out in the middle of nowhere, long distances from the load centers.

Daniel Sieberg: Indeed, this is where the country's wind blows the most, so-called Wind Alley. But this is where the majority of people live. So getting that power to the people would mean a massive, multi-billion-dollar grid restructuring. Plus, winds die down in summer, when demand is highest. Some turbines have been known to kill migratory birds, and not everyone welcomes such a sight in their backyard.

Jerry Tuttle: When I first came to west Texas, there was this, you know, cattle, and that was it, but now you see this and the sky's the limit.

Daniel Sieberg: But even those swept up in the winds of change admit that wind will only be one piece in the alternative energy puzzle. Daniel Sieberg, CBS News, Sweetwater, Texas.

UNIT 7

 A Culinary Art Canvas

Reporter: A Canadian student living in London found a surprising use for the food that we normally just throw away. Lauren Purnell is her name. She uses leftovers for her art and her photography. So she turns aging fruits and vegetables into a culinary canvas. Her work is a social media success and she has more than 46,000 followers on Tumblr. We visited her in her London apartment just to watch her work.

Lauren Purnell: We're on Portobello Road, known for its great food markets and fruit stalls, which is a bit of a dream for me. So my favorite is literally the stall right outside my door. It's probably about two feet outside the front step. I think it's such an inspiring place.

Where my piece begins, um, well sometimes it begins in the fridge, especially if something's about to go off and I don't want to throw it away, then I'll, you know, use that. So for instance, today, I'm going to use some leftover tarragon that I have that's not looking particularly healthy but that's going to look fantastic, um, as a photo. I was thinking this morning about what flowers I'd want to make, um, and I decided wildflowers because they're my favorite.

The other day when I was making salad, I realized that if you see the inside of the radish is a really nice white color as well. So I thought if I just took that skin off, then that would be perfect for constructing petals for my daisies so that's what I'm going to do. At this point, I think I'm going to find the middle, which I have a lemon that I used yesterday and actually am going to use the bit that's already a bit, you know, tarnished and banged up because that's going to make it look a lot more real as well.

When something's going off in the fridge and I don't want to throw it out, kind of put it there and be like, "What are you? What can we do with this?" Another really important consideration when I'm making my pieces is how the photo is going to turn out, so I tend to make all my pieces, um, either kind of early morning or late afternoon because if I get the wrong sunlight, then, you know, it won't capture the piece as it is. So I think that's probably, that's probably done, which means I get the blueberries.

UNIT 8

▶ Senior Exercise

Anchor: Exercise can help people of all ages, including aging seniors. Carter Evans shows us one gym that's helping older Americans find their strength.

Teacher: One, two —

Carter Evans (Reporter): This isn't your granddaughter's aerobics class.

Teacher: Three, right there and go.

Carter Evans: Call it a new twist.

Woman 1: Be careful.

Carter Evans: On an old art form. "Cane fu."

Mike Moreno: We turned the fitness equation on its head.

Carter Evans: Mike Moreno is CEO of Nifty after Fifty, a fitness chain that developed the class with a simple goal.

Mike Moreno: To actually make a senior feel powerful with something that normally represents frailty.

Berta Mayberry: Sometimes when they see you, they think, "Oh, poor thing."

Carter Evans: Berta Mayberry is 77 and anything but frail.

Berta Mayberry: I don't even walk like that. I walk like this so they know it's a weapon.

Carter Evans: The exercise itself is also a weapon, helping to prevent falls, which every year, send more than two million seniors to the emergency room. According to the Centers for Disease Control, only 35% of Americans over 65 are considered physically fit. The aches and pains take their toll, says 81-year-old Julianne Gooselaw.

Julianne Gooselaw: Five years ago, I broke my shoulder, and then I had a knee replacement a year ago.

Carter Evans: But with regular visits to the gym ...

Julianne Gooselaw: Now I can do almost a mile on the treadmill, where I couldn't do that two years ago but I can now. I'm stronger now than I've ever been.

Carter Evans: It's a boon for them.

Kim Bogue: I like to fight back.

Carter Evans: Not so much for those trying to mess with them. Carter Evans, CBS News, Los Angeles.

Name: _____ Date: _____

PART A KEY SKILLS
MAKING PREDICTIONS FROM A TEXT TYPE

1 You are going to read an essay. Before reading, look at Paragraph 1. Then check the statements you think will be true.

   1 The style of the writing will be formal. ☐
   2 The purpose of the text will be to entertain the reader. ☐
   3 The text will give factual information about a topic. ☐
   4 The text will ask you to imagine characters in a story. ☐
   5 The text will give instructions on how to do something. ☐

Read the essay and check your predictions.

English-Language Signs Around the World

1   You can not only *hear* the English language spoken in countries around the world, but you can also *see* it on signs everywhere, from Mexico to China. If you look around the streets of Tokyo, for example, you will find that Japanese is the most common language on signs. In fact, 99% of the Tokyo population speaks Japanese, but 20% of the signs in Tokyo are in English. Other studies have found similar patterns all over the world. Who, then, are these signs for?

2   Most people agree that English signs in other countries do not exist for the benefit of tourists. In Dubai, for example, English is visible in cafés, stores, and in ads. However, most tourists to Dubai come from non-English-speaking countries, such as India or Sri Lanka.

3   Many researchers now believe that English signs are not intended for English speakers. In fact, they "speak" to the local population. In Tokyo, for example, an English-language sign may include mistakes or may use English in a strange way. However, its message is usually understood by the target population: Japanese speakers.

4   One possible reason for the use of English in signs around the world is that many people think that English is exotic and fashionable. If English stops being fashionable, then these signs will probably disappear very quickly. Similarly, if you walk around London, you will find many cafés with Italian-language signs. These signs might not make sense to an Italian person, but that is not important. The signs are "speaking" to people in London who think that the Italian language and culture is fashionable.

5   Many researchers believe that, in fact, English is not replacing other languages culturally in these countries. A large number of English-language signs in a place like Tokyo, for example, does not mean that American or British culture is replacing Japanese. On the contrary, it shows that the Japanese language is so strong that the Japanese feel comfortable with displaying other languages in addition to their own.

TOPIC SENTENCES

2 Write the topic sentences for the paragraphs.

   1 Paragraph 2: _____
   2 Paragraph 3: _____
   3 Paragraph 4: _____
   4 Paragraph 5: _____

PART B ADDITIONAL SKILLS

3 Write *T* (true) or *F* (false) next to the statements. Correct the false statements.

_____ 1 The most visible language in Tokyo is English.

_____

_____ 2 According to the essay, these English-language signs are for the local population.

_____

_____ 3 The English-language signs in Tokyo sometimes contain language which might confuse native
          English speakers.

_____

_____ 4 In London, many people have a positive attitude toward Italian-language signs.

_____

_____ 5 The Japanese language is slowly dying out in Tokyo.

_____

Name: _____ Date: _____

PART A KEY VOCABULARY

1 Complete the sentences with the correct form of the words in the box.

| authenticity | convenience | discount | ensure | experiment | influence | relatively | situated |

1 Some people worry that big businesses have too much _____ on our government.
2 Because the farm is _____ in a valley, it is protected from strong winds.
3 Large supermarket chains can afford to offer _____ that smaller independent stores cannot afford to offer.
4 Since moving to the city, I have gotten used to the _____ of having food delivered in rainy weather so that I don't have to get wet.
5 The scientists are _____ with a new type of tomato that can grow in cold climates.
6 The store opened _____ recently—only about a month ago.
7 We really like the _____ of the food in this Thai restaurant. It tastes like they made it in Bangkok.
8 The company _____ that all orders will be shipped within twenty-four hours. If not, shipping is free.

2 Complete the text with the correct form of the words in the box.

| consumption | fresh | increase | ingredient | insist | perfectionist | selling point | specialty |

A big social question at the moment is this one: is it OK to eat something that was grown thousands of miles away? People often talk about the importance of food being (1) _____ , or not very old. Many people (2) _____ that the further food has traveled, the worse it is. They argue that as the distance between a food source and a consumer (3) _____ , the quality decreases. A true local food (4) _____ will tell you that you should limit your (5) _____ of food to products that come from within 50 miles of your home.

However, some of us have become very fond of certain imported foods. The main (6) _____ of a beautiful piece of French cheese is that it was made in France. Some food and drink (7) _____ , including certain types of coffee, cannot be produced everywhere. In addition, many of us use imported (8) _____ , such as olive oil, in our meals every day.

PART B LANGUAGE DEVELOPMENT
ACADEMIC ALTERNATIVES TO PHRASAL VERBS

3 Replace the phrasal verbs in parentheses with the correct form of the verbs in the box.

confuse	continue	exhaust	increase	remove

1 The number of people going abroad to find work has (gone up) _____ in recent years.
2 When the new government came into power, they (took away) _____ many of the old street signs and put up new ones.
3 My parents both speak different languages. I'm bilingual, but when I speak to them, I sometimes (mix up) _____ one word with another.
4 Some people predict that the world's supply of oil will be (used up) _____ in a few decades.
5 We cannot (go on) _____ polluting our lakes and rivers.

GLOBALIZATION VOCABULARY

4 Complete the article with the correct form of the words in the box.

consumption	diet	multinational	obesity	poverty

(1) _____ , or the condition of being extremely overweight, has doubled since 1980. It is now no longer confined to certain countries, like the United States, but has become a(n) (2) _____ problem. Multiple factors contribute to this condition. A(n) (3) _____ high in fat is one; the increased (4) _____ of sugary drinks is another. But another factor is also critically important: (5) _____ . Researchers have found that lower-income people are much more likely to be obese because they often cannot afford to buy healthier food.

Name: _____   Date: _____

PART A GRAMMAR FOR WRITING
NOUN PHRASES

1 Circle the correct words to complete the sentences.

    1 Social networking *sites / pages* are popular all over the world.
    2 It's just a fact of *modern / today's* life.
    3 The increased ability to work from home is a relatively *recent / old* development.
    4 Let's go eat at that *new Peruvian / Peruvian new* restaurant.
    5 The vegetables in our store come from *a number of / more than one* countries.

TIME PHRASES

2 Find and correct the mistakes in the sentences.

    1 At present time, the economy seems to be doing well.

    2 Historic, Canada has always been a multilingual country.

    3 More and more people have traveled abroad in recently years.

    4 Lila Moreno, who was former the CEO of PC International, will be the new head of Global Enterprises.

    5 We cannot rely on the same systems that we have used in the future.

PART B WRITING TASK

How has globalization changed the world of fashion and clothes?

3 Write an explanatory essay. Include an introductory paragraph with your thesis, at least two body paragraphs, and a concluding paragraph.

Name: _____   Date: _____

Read the essay. Then answer the questions that follow.

The Value of Higher Education?

1   Do schools really prepare young people for real life? There are many examples of successful people who never went to college. Similarly, are employers these days looking for people with qualifications in subjects like history or literature? Research seems to indicate that what employers are really looking for are people with experience, which traditionally is not part of a high school or college curriculum.

2   To illustrate one side of the argument, look at the example of an entrepreneur from Seattle who is now the director of a large electronics company. He dropped out of school when he was 17 and began working for his parents in their small office cleaning business. After a few weeks, he had saved $250. With this money, he began buying some small electronics and selling them at a local market. Today his fortune is estimated at $270 million.

3   Such examples show that many valuable skills can be acquired outside of the classroom. The ability to work hard and be self-disciplined is arguably more important than learning facts or memorizing poems. Regardless of whether or not a person has a degree, companies increasingly want employees with good communication or other "soft" skills, as well as certain qualifications. Of course, these skills can often be learned through experience in the real world.

4   However, schools do have an important role in preparing students for the world. As children spend time with other people in school, they learn how to interact in society and to respect rules and authority. As they progress into higher education, they learn how to manage time and how to deal with deadlines. They learn how to become independent and critical thinkers, how to express their opinions, and how to deal with complicated ideas. In summary, education is not only about facts and figures; it is also about developing important personal qualities.

5   In short, it is important to remember that few people will become millionaires by dropping out of school and selling electronics. Therefore, schools probably do prepare students for the real world because they give the majority the necessary tools to fit into society and because they allow more people to achieve success without relying on luck.

PART A KEY SKILLS
MAKING INFERENCES

1 Write *T* (true), *F* (false), or *DNS* (does not say) next to the statements. Explain why the false statements are false.

_____ 1 The Seattle entrepreneur could not get into college.
_____

_____ 2 The writer includes the example of the Seattle entrepreneur to show that traditional education is not always necessary to be successful.
_____

_____ 3 Employers do not want to hire people with qualifications anymore.
_____

_____ 4 The writer thinks that the most important benefit of schools is the knowledge of academic subjects that students get.
_____

_____ 5 Hundreds of millionaires in the U.S. do not have college degrees.
_____

PART B ADDITIONAL SKILLS

2 Write the correct paragraph number next to the descriptions.

    a General summary and conclusions _____
    b An example supporting the argument for a higher education _____
    c An explanation of what skills can be acquired outside school _____
    d An introduction to the topic of the essay _____
    e An example supporting the argument against a higher education _____

Prism 3 Reading and Writing © Cambridge University Press 2017 **Photocopiable**

Name: _____   Date: _____

PART A KEY VOCABULARY

1 Complete the sentences with the correct form of the words in the box.

> core principles   evolve   online degree   concrete   launch
> credible alternative   virtual classroom   underrepresented

1 We're learning about the _____ of American democracy, including individual rights, the consent of government, and the rule of law.
2 We have only recently _____ into a species that uses computers to communicate.
3 Charlotte is pursuing a(n) _____ in accounting from Cyber School.
4 Physics has some fascinating theories, but I prefer spending time in the lab solving _____ problems.
5 The school has just _____ a new program in emergency medical assistance, with the first students starting this semester.
6 A number of people are beginning to think that online classes offer a(n) _____ to traditional schools due to some positive results of studies.
7 Does a(n) _____ offer students the same opportunity to interact with each other as one that meets on campus?
8 Women now make up over half of all college students, but they are still _____ in technical schools where the majority of students are male.

2 Match the sentence halves. Use the words in bold to help you.

1 A major in college focuses on _____
2 Although many people consider **distance learning** to be _____
3 Although a college education can help women get better jobs, _____
4 After getting their first job after college, _____
5 Researchers are taking advantage of **technological advances** in 3D printing _____
6 While subjects like art and history are still popular, _____
7 She plans to **pursue** a degree in veterinary science _____

a to create inexpensive artificial limbs for people.
b it cannot erase the **gender gap** in the workplace overnight.
c many students are now more **oriented** toward science, technology, and math.
d subjects in a single department or **discipline**.
e after spending the summer working at an animal hospital.
f most graduates appreciate the **significant difference** between school and work life.
g a **modern phenomenon**, people have been taking courses by mail for centuries.

PART B LANGUAGE DEVELOPMENT
EDUCATION VOCABULARY

3 Circle the correct words in the sentences.

1 When you are a student at our university, you will have access to a wide range of academic *semesters / journals* online.

2 The student was found guilty of *plagiarism / assignment* when it was discovered that he copied most of his work from the Internet.

3 There are two *tutors / semesters*: one in the spring and one in the fall. You will complete three modules in each one.

4 It is important not just to attend but also to participate in the weekly a*ssignments / seminars* in order to pass this class.

5 You should begin thinking about the final *assignment / degree* for this class, which is to write a 5,000-word paper on a topic of your choice.

ACADEMIC WORDS

4 Complete the sentences with the correct form of the words in the box.

establishment	motivation	principle	significant	virtual

1 Studies have shown that having a college degree makes a(n) _____ difference in how much a person earns over their lifetime.

2 School can be difficult at any age if you don't have the _____ to do well.

3 April 14 marks the hundredth year since the _____ of the university's college of dentistry.

4 Our school was founded on the _____ that every child deserves a good education.

5 Although _____ courses are very popular these days, I prefer traditional ones with a professor and students in a classroom.

Prism 3 Reading and Writing © Cambridge University Press 2017 **Photocopiable**

Name: _____   Date: _____

PART A GRAMMAR FOR WRITING
TRANSITIONS TO SHOW COMPARISON AND CONTRAST

1 Complete the sentences with the comparison and contrast words in the box.

in contrast   however   on the other hand   similarly   unlike

1 My brother got a doctorate in microbiology. _____ , I left school and started working when I was 18.
2 In secondary school you have to take some courses you don't like. _____ , in college you have to take some core courses that you might not like.
3 In a seminar, _____ in lectures, you are allowed to ask questions and discuss things.
4 I would love to go to one of the top schools in the country. All of them, _____ , are too expensive for me.
5 Southfield offers great courses in engineering, but, _____ , it is not very strong in the arts.

ADVERB CLAUSES OF CONTRAST

2 Combine the sentences using *while* or *whereas*. More than one answer may be possible.

1 Austin College prepares students for business. Lakeland College prepares students for life.

_____
_____

2 Both of my parents want me to go to a good school. My mother wants me to choose a good school that is close to home.

_____
_____

3 The first two years of college are known for being difficult. The last two years of college are usually very enjoyable.

_____
_____

4 My science teacher is very serious. My history teacher is very entertaining.

_____
_____

5 Diablo Valley is a huge university. City Central is a small college.

_____
_____

PART B WRITING TASK

Discuss the similarities and differences between studying at a large school and a small one.

3 Write a comparison and contrast essay. Include an introductory paragraph with your thesis, 1–2 body paragraphs about similarities and differences, and a concluding paragraph with your opinion.

Name: _____   Date: _____

Read the article. Then answer the questions that follow.

Antibiotics: Helpful or Harmful?

1   According to a recent government report, one of the biggest dangers currently facing the world today comes from a medicine that has saved millions of lives: antibiotics. The widespread use of antibiotics has resulted in the growth of drug-resistant bacteria. Scientists warn us that infections caused by these new bacteria could become a catastrophic global threat in the near future.

2   Antibiotics revolutionized medicine when they were first discovered in the first half of the 20th century. Alexander Fleming was the first scientist to conduct research into antibiotics when he discovered penicillin in 1929. Since 1945, antibiotics have been widely used in the fight against potentially fatal infections, and this medicine has helped countless people around the world.

3   However, according to many researchers, antibiotics are now being overused. Doctors often prescribe them to patients even though they may not be necessary or even effective. In addition, farmers routinely add antibiotics to the feed they give their animals in the belief that this keeps their livestock healthy. These antibiotics eventually find their way into the human food supply, with sometimes dangerous results.

4   Despite the fact that antibiotics are unquestionably very effective against a number of diseases and have saved many lives, there is a risk involved in taking them, according to recent research. The problem is that every time a person takes antibiotics to combat an infection—or eats meat containing antibiotics—some bacteria are destroyed, but some also remain. These surviving bacteria can quickly grow and multiply, resulting in what scientists call *superinfections*. Superinfections, also known as *superbugs*, are caused by bacteria that have evolved to be resistant to some of the most common antibiotics.

5   Doctors in many parts of the world have seen the rise of new forms of tuberculosis and E-coli bacteria in the past ten years. Doctors warn that these new and very dangerous bacteria are becoming much more common, and that they may be much more difficult, or even impossible, to treat. According to some scientists, drug-resistant bacteria could become an even bigger problem for mankind than climate change unless we stop overusing antibiotics.

PART A KEY SKILLS
ANNOTATING A TEXT

1 Follow the steps to annotate the article. Then use your annotations to answer the questions.

- Highlight the topic sentence in each paragraph.
- Underline one important supporting detail in each paragraph.
- Put a box around two names for bacteria that are resistant to antibiotics.
- Circle two types of bacteria that are now a problem due to the overuse of antibiotics.

1 What global threat is the topic of the article?

_____

2 Who discovered the first important antibiotic? When?

_____

3 What are two ways that antibiotics are being overused?

_____

4 What are bacteria that have become resistant to antibiotics called?

_____

5 What examples of bacteria that have become a problem due to the overuse of antibiotics does the writer mention?

_____

PART B ADDITIONAL SKILLS

2 Circle the correct answers to complete the sentences.

1 *Drug-resistant bacteria* refers to bacteria that …
   a are not affected by medicine.
   b are destroying medicine.
   c cannot fight medicine.

2 Antibiotics have the ability to …
   a fight medicine.
   b feed livestock.
   c save lives.

3 Antibiotics are …
   a not just consumed by patients.
   b used by doctors only when necessary.
   c always very effective.

4 The overuse of antibiotics is helping …
   a destroy bacteria.
   b bacteria change and become stronger.
   c patients resist infections.

5 It is possible that in the future …
   a bacteria could cause climate change.
   b doctors will refuse to treat tuberculosis.
   c some bacteria may be impossible to treat.

Name: _____   Date: _____

PART A KEY VOCABULARY

1 Complete the sentences with the correct form of the words in the box.

| consultation   controversial   conventional   proponent   safety net   surgery   symptom |

1   Ali had all the _____ of a cold: a sore throat, congestion, and a cough.
2   Even doctors who usually practice _____ medicine are now trying alternatives such as acupuncture.
3   The doctor told me not to eat or drink fluids for eight hours before my _____ .
4   The issue of using animals in scientific experiments has become very _____ in recent years.
5   As a vegetarian, Julio is a strong _____ of eating lots of fruit and vegetables to stay healthy.
6   Many people believe that it is a government's responsibility to provide a _____ to help protect its citizens when they lose their jobs or health insurance.
7   After I fell and hurt my knee, my doctor recommend that I schedule a _____ with a specialist to figure out the best treatment.

2 Read the sentences. Match the words in bold and their definitions.

1   My brother has been getting **treatment** for his asthma for two years now. _____
2   The government agreed to **fund** the research and development of a new cancer drug. _____
3   Researchers believe that years of hard **labor** may increase the risk of heart problems. _____
4   Her grandparents refuse to move in with her because they don't want to be a **burden** to her. _____
5   The study found that mosquitos are the **chief** cause of the spread of the Zika virus. _____
6   I always catch a cold in the winter, **regardless** of what I do to stay healthy. _____
7   The cough medicine the doctor gave me was a thick, bad-tasting **substance**. _____
8   The family gave a **contribution** to the children's hospital in honor of their daughter. _____

a   a duty or responsibility that is hard to bear
b   money, support, or other help
c   practical work, especially work that involves physical effort
d   the use of drugs, exercises, etc. to improve or cure the condition of a sick or injured person
e   a material with particular physical characteristics
f   despite; not being affected by something
g   to provide money to pay for something
h   most important or main

PART B LANGUAGE DEVELOPMENT
MEDICAL VOCABULARY

3 Complete the sentences with the correct form of the words in the box.

> drug dependency   epidemic   patent   preventable illness   sedentary lifestyle

1 A(n) _____ is a disease, like influenza, that spreads to a very large number of people in a short period of time.
2 The likelihood of obesity increases if you have a(n) _____ , which is why it is important to make exercise part of your daily routine.
3 A(n) _____ is one that can be avoided by getting a vaccine or having a healthier lifestyle.
4 Addiction to sleeping pills is a type of _____ .
5 In the United States, a(n) _____ gives a pharmaceutical company the exclusive right to produce and market a drug for 20 years.

ACADEMIC VOCABULARY

4 Choose the best words to complete the sentences.

1 Surgeons need to work with great _____ during an operation.
   a patients   **b** precision   **c** profession
2 If you want to work in the _____ profession, you will need to train for a number of years.
   a medicine   **b** medication   **c** medical
3 That drug is _____ ; it was banned by the government ten years ago.
   a alternative   **b** illegal   **c** adverse
4 Nurses often have to work under _____ conditions, such as spending long hours in overcrowded hospitals.
   a adverse   **b** precise   **c** adversity
5 People in this area of the country do not have access to _____ health care. In fact, several towns have no doctors.
   a adequate   **b** complex   **c** physical

Name: _____ Date: _____

PART A GRAMMAR FOR WRITING
ARTICLES

1 Complete the sentences with *a, an*, or *the*. If no article is needed, write Ø.

   1 The doctor prescribed _____ antibiotic for my ear infection.
   2 One of the biggest problems with doctors is that they are often too busy to spend much time with _____ patients.
   3 What he needs right now is _____ rest and relaxation.
   4 I am having surgery on my foot tomorrow. After that, I will take _____ week or two off from work.
   5 Most governments recognize that obesity is a growing problem in _____ world today.

TRANSITIONS TO SHOW CONCESSION

2 Complete the sentences with the correct words or phrases in the box. Some sentences may have more than one answer.

despite   despite the fact that   even though   in spite of   nevertheless

   1 _____ smoking is known to be unhealthy, many people find it difficult to give up.
   2 I started running three times a week. _____ , I am still finding it hard to lose weight.
   3 Some doctors are still prescribing this drug _____ its risks.
   4 _____ the government's warning, people are still taking too many antibiotics.
   5 _____ I eat well and exercise regularly, I still get sick at least twice a year.

PART B WRITING TASK

> Should unhealthy activities, like smoking, drinking soda, or eating fast food, be illegal?

3 Write an opinion essay. Include an introductory paragraph with your thesis, 1–2 body paragraphs with your arguments and supporting evidence, and a concluding paragraph.

Name: _____   Date: _____

Read the article. Then answer the questions that follow.

Predicting the Next Tsunami

1   When a devastating tsunami hit the island of Sri Lanka in December 2005, it caught people by surprise. An earthquake had struck beneath the Indian Ocean, and no one was able to predict the catastrophe in time. However, according to many witnesses, animals somehow knew what was happening long before humans did. Elephants were seen running away from the ocean, and birds such as flamingos were noticeably upset. One Sri Lankan remembers bats flying away just before the tsunami struck. And at Yala National Park on the southern Sri Lankan coast, very few dead animals were found despite the park being home to leopards, elephants, bears, and hundreds of other large animals.

2   This strange behavior has led some people to ask whether animals have some kind of sixth sense—an ability to understand what is happening without using the traditional senses, such as hearing or sight. Or, perhaps, the senses of animals are more sensitive than human senses. If animals are able to predict, or sense ahead of time, a change in the environment, might they be able to provide humans with an early warning about disasters?

3   Another catastrophic tsunami struck Japan in 2011. It, too, was caused by a massive earthquake that measured 9.0 on the Richter scale. Not only did it cause immediate, large-scale devastation; when it hit the Fukushima nuclear power plant, the country was forced to deal with a major environmental disaster as well. Although there were no reports of animals running away from the ocean before this tsunami, the Japanese city of Susaki has since debated whether or not to try out an early-warning system that involves animals. According to various reports, birds such as chickens have been seen getting excited just before large earthquakes. Cats and dogs have also been observed behaving in unusual ways before such events. The mayor of Susaki has thought about asking residents to prepare themselves if they notice animals suddenly behaving in a strange way.

4   However, as yet, there is no reliable scientific evidence that animals really can sense when a disaster is about to strike. Because of this, the Japanese government has decided, for the moment, not to base important decisions on the way some animals might behave. Scientists at the United States Geological Survey (USGS) note that studies to establish a link between this kind of animal behavior and earthquakes is difficult to carry out. On the other hand, the USGS has not investigated such a link since the 1970s, so perhaps it is time to do so.

PART A KEY SKILLS
IDENTIFYING COHESIVE DEVICES

1   Find the words from the left column in the article. Match them to the ideas they refer to in the right column. You will not use all of the ideas.

1 Paragraph 1: *it* _____
2 Paragraph 2: *This strange behavior* _____
3 Paragraph 3: *it* _____
4 Paragraph 3: *they* _____
5 Paragraph 4: *Because of this* _____

a lack of scientific evidence
b animals
c a tsunami in 2005
d residents of Susaki, Japan
e a tsunami in 2011
f running or flying away; being very upset

PART B ADDITIONAL SKILLS

2 Write the number of the paragraph that matches the main idea.

    a the question of a link between animal behavior and disasters _____

    b the lack of scientific evidence for animal prediction _____

    c Japanese reactions to earthquakes _____

    d strange animal behavior before a tsunami in Sri Lanka _____

3 Read the questions. Circle the inferences that can be made from the article.

    1 What does the writer think is strange about the tsunami of 2005?

      a It caught people by surprise.

      b Animals acted upset before anything seemed to happen.

    2 What does the writer think is true about animals?

      a They have the same number of senses as humans.

      b Their senses may be superior to those of humans.

    3 What conclusion would the writer probably agree with?

      a We need to study animals more closely in order to understand their reactions.

      b Governments will soon use animals to predict disasters.

Name: _____   Date: _____

PART A KEY VOCABULARY

1   Complete the radio broadcast with the correct form of the words in the box.

casualty   community   crucial   devastating   disrupt   measure   monitor   rely on

---

HURRICANE ALERT

Hurricane Olivia is now headed toward the (1) _____ of West Shores in Florida. The hurricane struck Haiti on Wednesday, where (2) _____ floods destroyed several towns and (3) _____ power to thousands of homes for more than 18 hours. Haiti has reported 23 (4) _____ , including several deaths, as of 11 p.m. Saturday. Authorities stress that it is (5) _____ that all West Shores residents take the proper (6) _____ to protect themselves and their homes. You can (7) _____ national radio and television to (8) _____ the progress of the storm and keep you updated.

---

2   Complete the paragraph with the correct form of the words in the box.

criticize   identify   infrastructure   issue   maintenance   policy   reduction   strategy

The city council has (1) _____ several problems that we need to address this year. The first (2) _____ is that much of our (3) _____ , including our roads and bridges, is badly in need of (4) _____ , and several bridges need to be replaced completely. We know that it is very easy to (5) _____ ideas for improving conditions, having already received a number of negative responses to the solutions we suggested last month. Yet, it is much harder to think of new (6) _____ for solving these problems. We welcome all suggestions from the public but ask that you follow our official (7) _____ for submitting emails, which can be found on our website. We hope that this will lead to a(n) (8) _____ of negative emails that do not help us solve the city's problems.

PART B LANGUAGE DEVELOPMENT
ACADEMIC NOUN PHRASES

3 Rewrite the phrases in the left column of the table as academic noun phrases.

a report written by the government	1
to mitigate a disaster	2
to reduce risk	3
to protect against floods	4
the act of manufacturing products	5
the act of analyzing risks	6

NATURAL DISASTER VOCABULARY

4 Choose the best word to complete the collocations in the sentences.

1 The 2011 Japanese tsunami was a _____ disaster which affected millions of people.
   a major   **b** long-term   **c** seasonal

2 Southeast Asia experiences a number of _____ disasters, such as floods, every year.
   a prolonged   **b** natural   **c** controlled

3 The new dam is a(n) _____ project that involves engineers from four different countries.
   a severe   **b** terrible   **c** ambitious

4 Because the region has suffered a(n) _____ drought for the past two years, the agricultural economy has been devastated.
   a natural   **b** large-scale   **c** extreme

5 Several towns in Slovakia and Hungary experienced _____ flooding when the Danube River overflowed last year.
   a severe   **b** natural   **c** ambitious

Name: _____ Date: _____

PART A GRAMMAR FOR WRITING
EXPRESSING SOLUTIONS WITH IT

1 Write sentences using the words provided and an expression with *it*.

1 important / prepare / natural disasters
It _____

2 surprising / more people didn't know / the tsunami
It _____

3 worth / remember / earthquakes / happen at any time
It _____

4 good idea / prepare for emergencies
It _____

5 sad fact / so many homes / destroyed in the hurricane
It _____

PART B WRITING TASK

Write a report that provides both short- and long-term solutions to local air or water pollution and takes the costs into consideration.

2 Write a report. Describe the problem and main purpose of the report in the introductory paragraph. Write at least two body paragraphs with recommended solutions. Summarize and evaluate your key points in the concluding paragraph.

Name: _____   Date: _____

PART A KEY SKILLS
SKIMMING A TEXT

1 Skim the article. Check the five opinions mentioned by the writer.

 1 Modern Dubai looks very different than it did in the past. ☐
 2 Many tourists enjoy visiting famous skyscrapers. ☐
 3 Most Tokyo residents do not like older styles of architecture. ☐
 4 Prague spends a lot of money preserving its older buildings. ☐
 5 There should be more shopping malls in the Italian capital of Rome. ☐
 6 The old buildings of Rome have great historical significance. ☐
 7 The Eiffel Tower was not admired by everyone when it was first built. ☐

Urban Architecture: Positive or Negative?

1   Throughout history, cities have always changed and grown. As the human population expands, cities need to get bigger, and often taller. Some of the most famous buildings in the world are also the tallest: the 2,723-feet-high (830 meters) Burj Khalifa in Dubai or the twin Petronas Towers in Kuala Lumpur are some examples. In the Western hemisphere, the tallest building is the relatively new One World Trade Center in New York City, at 1,776 feet (541 meters). However, rapid urban development comes at a price. Many old buildings in cities like Kuala Lumpur, Singapore, or New York City have disappeared, replaced by luxury hotels, skyscrapers, and shopping centers. Some places like Dubai have changed beyond recognition in the last 20 years.

2   However, is this a bad thing? After all, beautiful new skyscrapers and shopping malls do attract tourists. Also, for residents, it is not always safe to live beside old buildings. In places like Tokyo, there are very few old buildings, most having been destroyed by fires or earthquakes. In addition, the smaller size of older buildings makes them less suitable for housing the growing populations of most cities. The cost of maintaining old buildings can often be high, especially in cities like Prague that have extensive, old downtown areas.

3   On the other hand, some old buildings do have enormous cultural importance. There are few people who would suggest tearing down the ancient buildings of Rome to build new shopping malls or office buildings. Such constructions are priceless. Not only are they beautiful, but they tell us a great deal about how past generations lived. We have to take responsibility for preserving important buildings so that future generations can enjoy and learn from them.

4   In conclusion, it is difficult to argue that we should forbid the creation of new buildings. Cities do change and evolve over time. Of course, not everyone appreciates modern architecture, but it is worth bearing in mind that when the famous Eiffel Tower of Paris was opened in 1889, it was widely criticized as useless and monstrous. Each generation creates its own architectural styles, and these should be encouraged and appreciated. In short, we need to be able to expand our cities in a way that respects the architecture of the past but also welcomes the future.

Prism 3 Reading and Writing © Cambridge University Press 2017 **Photocopiable**

PART B ADDITIONAL SKILLS

2 Match the sentences from the article to the correct paraphrases.

1 However, this rapid development comes at a price. _____
2 In addition, the smaller size of older buildings makes them less suitable for housing the growing populations of most cities. _____
3 On the other hand, some old buildings do have enormous cultural importance. _____
4 There are few people who would suggest tearing down the ancient buildings of Rome to build a new shopping mall. _____
5 We have to take responsibility for preserving important buildings so that future generations can enjoy and learn from them. _____
6 Each generation creates its own architectural styles, and these should be encouraged and appreciated. _____
7 In short, we need to be able to expand our cities in a way that respects the architecture of the past but also welcomes the future. _____

a It is our job to save old buildings for our children and grandchildren to appreciate.
b We need to recognize and respect the fact that building styles change over time.
c The modernization of urban areas is not completely positive.
d We ultimately need to find a compromise between preserving existing architecture and developing cities.
e Also, older buildings cannot meet the demands of today's urban populations.
f However, historical architecture is a significant expression of a culture.
g Most people agree that it would be ridiculous to replace structures like the Colosseum or the Pantheon with modern stores.

3 Write the paraphrase from Exercise 2 that best states the writer's conclusion about the positive and negative effects of urban architecture.

_____

UNIT 5 LANGUAGE QUIZ

Name: _____ Date: _____

PART A KEY VOCABULARY

1 Complete the sentences with the correct form of the words in the box.

| compromise   depressing   durable   efficiency   relevant   reputation   secondhand |

1 This company has a(n) _____ for building very expensive apartment buildings, so it was a surprise when they announced an affordable housing project.
2 One of the goals of the design firm is to increase the energy _____ and to reduce the operating costs of their new buildings.
3 The city's plans for building a highway are _____ to us because we are considering buying a home in that area.
4 I wanted a house in the country and my husband wanted to buy an apartment in the city. We reached a(n) _____ and bought a home in the suburbs with a big yard.
5 Some people find these old houses dark and _____ , but I think they are charming and fun.
6 My cousin always buys _____ furniture for his house from a thrift store or at a garage sale.
7 The builder explained that a metal roof is more _____ than wood, which only lasts about 15 years.

2 Complete the paragraph with the correct form of the words in the box.

| civilized   conservation   demonstrate   function   inspiring   reflect on   sector |

The (1) _____ of the historic district in our city is a matter of great importance to all of us on the Historic Preservation Committee. We share the belief that a(n) (2) _____ society respects its past. Many of these older buildings are (3) _____ examples of values that we still hold dear. For example, the (4) _____ of our original library was, and still is, to educate and enrich all (5) _____ of the population: rich and poor, young and old. Today I would like us to take a moment to (6) _____ what this committee has accomplished in the past year. Your efforts (7) _____ a remarkable passion for preserving history.

PART B LANGUAGE DEVELOPMENT
ACADEMIC WORD FAMILIES

3 Complete the sentences with the correct form of the words in parentheses.

1 We are concerned about the _____ impact of the new shopping mall. (environment)
2 The building has a very _____ appearance and obviously was not designed to be attractive. (function)
3 I work more _____ when I am at home. (efficient)
4 Everyone who works in this building says that it is _____ . One problem is that it has very few windows. (depress)
5 If we want to construct skyscrapers, then we should do it _____ , rather than destroying hundreds of old buildings to build one new tower. (responsible)
6 Walls of glass did not become a popular _____ style in the U.S. until the 1970s. (architecture)

ARCHITECTURE AND PLANNING VOCABULARY

4 Choose the best words to complete the sentences.

1 The corporation moved its offices outside the city to a(n) _____ location because it was less expensive.
   a urban   **b** suburban   **c** green

2 The government should consider having a(n) _____ around the city to prevent urban sprawl. We simply cannot allow more and more buildings to be constructed.
   a green belt   **b** environment   **c** skyscraper

3 The factory is on the _____ of the city, so it takes an hour to get there from downtown.
   a green belt   **b** outskirts   **c** urban sprawl

4 The hotel only offers very basic _____ , such as a small breakfast room and a 24-hour coffee machine.
   a amenities   **b** architecture   **c** outskirts

5 They had to bring in a(n) _____ to analyze how many floors the building could support.
   a environmentalist   **b** software engineer   **c** structural engineer

Name: _____   Date: _____

PART A GRAMMAR FOR WRITING
REGISTER IN ACADEMIC WRITING

1 Write academic synonyms from the box for the words and phrases in parentheses.

| approximately   calculate   considerable   critical   fundamentally   have a positive impact on |
| justified   of no benefit to   significant number   undoubtedly |

1 It is _____ (extremely important) that we plan for population increases in our city.
2 We urgently need to _____ (figure out) how much it will cost to renovate this building.
3 There is _____ (for sure) a competition among countries over who can build the tallest skyscraper.
4 It seems that there is a(n) _____ (large amount) of people who would prefer to preserve old, historical buildings.
5 _____ (Basically), the problem is that there are too many people and not enough places for them to live.
6 It is not clear that the costs of installing solar panels on a building are _____ (worth it).
7 There are _____ (about) 38 million people living in the greater Tokyo area.
8 A new skyscraper can _____ (be good for) a city's image.
9 Destroying old buildings is _____ (not at all good for) our national culture.
10 You need to invest a(n) _____ (very large) amount of money to create any kind of large building.

PART B WRITING TASK

What new building does your school need the most?

2 Write a persuasive essay. Include an introductory paragraph with your thesis, at least two body paragraphs with arguments for your choice, and a concluding paragraph.

Name: _____   Date: _____

Read the article. Then answer the questions that follow.

The Next Alternative Energy Source?

1   Most people are aware that fossil fuels are problematic. Not only are we running out of these resources, but they also contribute to global pollution and climate change. Furthermore, most of us are familiar with alternative, renewable power sources, which aim to capture energy from the sun, the wind, or water. However, here is one unusual idea you may not have heard of.

2   There are more than seven billion people living in the world, and most of us physically move around throughout the day. Scientists have known for a long time that electricity can be produced whenever **pressure** is applied to an object, for example, with a footstep. Therefore, if buildings or streets were equipped with **sensitive** floors, then a large amount of energy could be produced from people's footsteps. This type of energy is called *piezoelectricity*. (*Piezo* comes from the Greek word for "press.")

3   One footstep alone cannot generate a great deal of power. According to research, a single footstep produces enough energy to keep a small light bulb working for just one second. However, around 28,500 footsteps would be enough to operate an electric train for one second. If we consider that over 750,000 people walk through Grand Central Station in New York City every day—and one million during holidays—then it becomes clear that a large amount of power could be generated by this foot traffic.

4   This idea may seem unusual, but two train stations in Japan are already using this technology: Shibuya Station and Tokyo Station. The traffic in Shibuya Station is even greater than in Grand Central. About two million people walk through the station every day. Piezoelectric floors were installed in both of the Japanese train stations in 2007. Since then, the foot traffic has generated all the electricity needed to run the automatic ticket gates and the electronic display systems.

5   Piezoelectric floors have proven useful in smaller applications as well. Some nightclubs in the Netherlands and the United Kingdom have already constructed motion-sensitive dance rooms. Each floor contains crystals that produce electricity when they are pressed. As you can imagine, the large number of people dancing in these clubs results in a lot of piezoelectricity, which is then fed to nearby batteries to power the nightclub. Although these "eco-discos" are not powered completely by alternative means, they have significantly reduced their energy bills.

6   Will piezoelectricity become a major source of energy in the future? Some companies are exploring its use in a number of consumer electronic devices, such as cell phones and printers. Others are looking at using it in musical devices, including microphones and speakers. Several companies are also experimenting with its application in clocks and watches. Given the rapid rate of development in technology, we can expect many more new uses of piezoelectric power in the future.

PART A KEY SKILLS
WORKING OUT MEANING FROM CONTEXT

1 Find the words in bold in the article. Use the context to match them to their meanings.

1 **pressure** _____	a to produce
2 **sensitive** _____	b movement
3 **generate** _____	c the force produced when one object pushes against another
4 **footstep** _____	d the action of a person's foot touching the ground
5 **operate** _____	e easily changed or affected by something
6 **motion** _____	f to make something work

PART B ADDITIONAL SKILLS

2 Write the corresponding paragraph number next to its purpose.

    a Explains how a significant amount of energy could be produced _____

    b Shows how the technology can be applied on a smaller scale _____

    c Considers the future of the technology _____

    d Gives examples of how the technology is used on a larger scale _____

    e Explains the principle behind the technology _____

    f Introduces a new source of alternative energy _____

3 Write *T* (true), *F* (false), or *DNS* (does not say) next to the statements. Correct the false statements.

_____   **1** Most fossil fuels pollute the environment.

_____

_____   **2** Although the concept of piezoelectricity is interesting, footsteps generate very little power.

_____

_____   **3** The piezoelectric floors in Grand Central Station power the electronic displays in the station.

_____

_____   **4** Eco-discos in the Netherlands use several alternative energy sources, including piezoelectricity, to reduce their energy bills.

_____

_____   **5** Companies are testing the use of piezoelectricity to power small devices, like cell phones, watches, and speakers.

_____

_____   **6** Piezoelectricity is expected to become a major source of energy in the future.

_____

Name: _____ Date: _____

PART A KEY VOCABULARY

1 Complete the news report with the correct form of the words in the box.

address	aquatic	diminish	generate	offshore	resistant	urgent	vital

Earlier today the president [1] _____ reporters at a televised press conference. He spoke about a(n) _____ matter, one that he says can no longer be ignored without serious environmental consequences: the impact of [3] _____ drilling on the nation's marine wildlife. These drilling operations [4] _____ high levels of a variety of toxins in the water, which have killed a number of [5] _____ species, including fish, birds, and mammals. He pointed out that oil spills and leaks from drilling have greatly [6] _____ the sea turtle population so that they are now on the endangered species list. Oil in the ocean also damages the water-[7] _____ fur that normally protects seals and otters, causing these mammals to suffer and even die. Because scientist consider these creatures to be [8] _____ to the health of the nation's oceans and to the important fishing industry, the president has proposed an end to all future oil-drilling permits in these areas.

2 Complete the sentences with the correct form of the words in the box.

adopt	alarming	inexhaustible	initial	instigate	universal	utilize

1 Because Earth's resources are not _____ , we must conserve them.
2 There has been a(n) _____ increase in health problems due to air pollution, with 50% more cases of lung cancer this year than last year.
3 The committee voted to _____ the new regulations on auto emissions, which will go into effect November 1.
4 Solar panels _____ one of our great, free resources: sunlight.
5 Keith loves to _____ arguments, but he never wins them.
6 Dr. Chan's _____ research indicates that the polar ice caps are melting faster than we previously thought.
7 Most countries provide _____ health care, so that all of their citizens have access to the medical care they need.

PART B LANGUAGE DEVELOPMENT
ENERGY COLLOCATIONS

3 Choose the correct words to complete the sentences.

1 Industrial _____ is one of the leading causes of global warming.
  a energy   **b** pollution   **c** fuel

2 Oil _____ has actually increased in the past ten years.
  a production   **b** fuel   **c** energy

3 The rise of renewable _____ of energy will reduce our dependence on oil and coal.
  a fuels   **b** problems   **c** sources

4 Las Vegas now uses only renewable energy rather than fossil _____ to power its city government.
  a production   **b** fuels   **c** problem

5 An oil rig explosion in 2010 caused major environmental _____ in the Gulf of Mexico.
  a problems   **b** sources   **c** productions

FORMAL AND INFORMAL ACADEMIC VERBS

4 Complete the sentences with the correct form of the formal verbs in the box. Use the informal synonyms in parentheses to help you.

consult	contest	deliver	diminish	utilize

1 Oil and coal reserves are _____ rapidly. (decrease)
2 The president _____ a speech on renewable energy last night. (give)
3 Fewer people are _____ the need for renewable energy sources. (disagree with)
4 After _____ the engineer, we decided to install the solar panels on our garage. (talk with)
5 The engine in the hybrid car _____ 50% gas and 50% electricity. (use)

Name: _____ Date: _____

PART A GRAMMAR FOR WRITING
RELATIVE CLAUSES

1 Underline the relative clause in each sentence and choose the correct relative pronoun.

1 As far as I know, there are few people *who / which* can live without electricity.
2 It wasn't Tokyo, but Sendai *that / where* was hit by the tsunami.
3 I studied environmental science *which / when* I was in college.
4 It is not desirable to build wind turbines in areas *where / whose* large numbers of people live.
5 Several thousand people, *whose / who* homes were near the new dam, had to be relocated.

2 Complete the sentences with the correct relative pronoun. Then add commas to the sentences that contain nonidentifying relative clauses.

1 The cost of solar panels _____ many people think is excessive is expected to go down in the near future.
2 Offshore wind turbines _____ are generally very large can produce significant amounts of electricity.
3 Geothermal energy is energy _____ is generated and stored underground.
4 The famous actor _____ just made a new movie is a vocal supporter of solar energy.
5 People _____ drive old, inefficient cars should have to pay a tax.
6 The wealthy entrepreneur _____ Caribbean island is powered by solar energy spoke about the advantages of alternative power.

PART B WRITING TASK

What are two energy-efficient types of transportation? Discuss the advantages and disadvantages of both, and decide which one would work best for your city or country.

3 Write an essay. Include an introductory paragraph with your thesis, a body paragraph about each type of transportation, and a concluding paragraph with your preferred option and why.

Name: _____ Date: _____

PART A KEY SKILLS
SCANNING TO FIND INFORMATION

1 Scan the essay. Write the number of the paragraph in which each point is discussed.

a Graffiti artists do not respect private property. _____
b Artistic skill is necessary to create graffiti. _____
c Ancient graffiti tells us about life in the past. _____
d Graffiti artists can express important ideas. _____
e Self-expression is a right. _____
f Graffiti is always a crime. _____
g Graffiti that does not improve a city is the same as vandalism. _____

Graffiti: Art or Vandalism?

1   Graffiti exists in almost every city in the world. The word *graffiti* comes from the Italian *graffiato*, which means "scratched." Indeed, some of the earliest forms of graffiti can be found in ancient Roman sites. The ruins of Pompeii, in southern Italy, contain a large quantity of 2,000-year-old graffiti that is of great historical significance. However, in the modern world, graffiti has become something that is generally thought to be negative, and governments spend a great deal of time and money trying to remove it from walls and other publicly visible surfaces in towns and cities. Nevertheless, the question remains: should graffiti be considered an art form?

2   There are some who argue that graffiti is artistic because it requires as much creativity and artistic skill as any other art form. It may not appeal to everybody, they say, but not all people share the same aesthetic notions. After all, what is beautiful to one person may seem ugly to another. Graffiti is usually the work of someone trying to express their feelings and personality and, furthermore, it usually tries to send a message to other people. It is this message that sometimes makes a graffiti artist famous. The English graffiti artist Bansky gained fame for the political and social themes expressed in his works. He once said, "If you don't own a train company, then you go and paint on one instead." In other words, he believes that graffiti is an important expression of the social struggle between classes in a society.

3   There is, of course, an opposing point of view. Perhaps the most important argument against graffiti is that it uses public spaces illegally without permission. In other words, graffiti artists use someone else's property as their "canvas." Critics of graffiti argue that art should be about creation, not destruction. They maintain that graffiti destroys the appearance of beautiful buildings and makes whole towns and cities look uglier, which can lead to an increase in crime.

4   In the end, there seems to be one main question regarding graffiti, and that concerns the artists. Do these people have the right to express their feelings in public? In a free, democratic society the answer is yes—artists should be free to express themselves. However, art should not destroy what is already beautiful. If modern graffiti does not improve its "canvas"—the walls, bridges, and other structures on which it is painted, then it cannot be considered art. Instead, it is vandalism and is no more creative than breaking windows or destroying public buildings.

PART B ADDITIONAL SKILLS

2 Write the paragraph number next to the topic.

    a Arguments against graffiti _____
    b A background of graffiti _____
    c The writer's opinion of graffiti _____
    d Arguments for graffiti _____

3 Write *T* (true), *F* (false), or *DNS* (does not say) next to the statements. Correct the false statements.

_____   1 The word *graffiti* comes from Spanish.

_____

_____   2 There is a financial cost for cities to remove graffiti.

_____

_____   3 Some graffiti has a political message.

_____

_____   4 Banksy's graffiti makes public spaces more beautiful.

_____

_____   5 The writer feels that graffiti artists always have the right to use public property to express themselves.

_____

Name: _____   Date: _____

PART A KEY VOCABULARY

1 Choose the best word to complete each sentence.

1 According to this definition, *conceptual / contemporary* art is art that is being created now in our lifetime.
2 It is very difficult for me to see the *distinction / significance* between these two colors. They look the same to me.
3 Hector has the *significance / notion* that any form of self-expression is art.
4 For *established / conceptual* artists, the idea behind a work of art matters more than the work itself.
5 To be a good sculptor, you need to have good *cynical / mechanical* skills as well as artistic talent.
6 These cute drawings of kittens and puppies seem *cynical / banal* to me. I prefer art that is more unusual and thoughtful.
7 The *significance / notion* of graffiti in the world of art can be seen in recent exhibitions by important art museums.
8 You cannot expect the artist's parents to be *objective / banal* about their daughter's art.

2 Complete the sentences with the correct form of the words in the box.

acknowledge   aesthetic   analogous   cynical   established   perceive   sophisticated

1 In order to be successful, an interior designer needs a strong _____ sense.
2 Mona likes simple, common colors whereas I prefer more _____ , complex tones.
3 Trevor has become very _____ about the art market because he is having trouble selling his work.
4 The museum only buys works from older, _____ artists rather than those by younger, lesser known artists.
5 Becoming a Hollywood star is _____ to winning the lottery: both are extremely unlikely.
6 One of Edward Hopper's strengths was his ability to _____ beauty in ordinary scenes.
7 The talent of many great artists, such as Van Gogh and Gauguin, was not _____ during their lifetimes. They only became famous after their deaths.

PART B LANGUAGE DEVELOPMENT
PARAPHRASING

3 Circle the correct paraphrase for each sentence.

1 During his lifetime, El Greco was very misunderstood. Many people were puzzled by his dramatic and imaginative creations.
   a El Greco's work was considered dramatic during his lifetime.
   b Many of El Greco's contemporaries did not understand his work.
2 It was only following his death that Vermeer was recognized by the art world and the public for his art.
   a Vermeer only achieved recognition for his work after his death.
   b Following his death, Vermeer recognized the art world and public in his works.
3 When Monet started painting landscapes, he began experimenting with new, delicate colors and fascinating techniques like short brushstrokes.
   a Monet began experimenting with new worlds of delicate colors and short brushstrokes.
   b Monet used new colors and techniques in his landscapes.
4 In this painting the differences between light and dark colors are clearly displayed.
   a This painting contrasts light and dark colors.
   b This painting displays light and dark colors.

VOCABULARY FOR ART AND DESIGN

4 Complete the sentences with the adjectives in the box. Use the words and phrases in parentheses to help you.

> abstract   avant-garde   expressive   lifelike   monumental   moving

1 I'm sorry, but these paintings are too _____ for my taste. I prefer more traditional art. (modern and original)

2 Picasso's painting *Guernica* is considered a(n) _____ achievement in the history of political art. (very big or important)

3 Gustave Courbet liked to paint _____ scenes, showing real people in ordinary situations doing normal activities. (realistic)

4 The art of painters like Mark Rothko or Jackson Pollock is too _____ for me—I can't understand it. I prefer realistic landscape paintings and traditional photographs. (not concrete or realistic)

5 The movie was very _____ for me. I cried several times. (emotional)

6 Just look at the child in this painting—her face is so _____ . (showing what someone thinks or feels)

Name: _____ Date: _____

PART A GRAMMAR FOR WRITING
SUBSTITUTION

1 Match the sentences.

1 Many people hate graffiti. _____
2 Michelangelo's sculpture *David* is five meters tall. _____
3 Picasso completed his enormous painting *Guernica* in 1937. _____
4 Calligraphy is the art of pen and ink. _____
5 Cartier-Bresson was a famous French photographer. _____

a The large mural by the Spanish artist can now be seen in Madrid, Spain.
b However, the fact that this controversial painting style is disliked does not make it illegal.
c The statue by the Italian artist can be seen in Florence.
d This beautiful writing is popular in many Asian and Arab countries.
e Pictures taken by him are exhibited in art museums around the world.

ELLIPSIS

2 Cross out the words that are not needed to avoid repetition in the sentences.

1 Some art is easy to understand, but a lot is not easy to understand.
2 I like abstract art, but my wife does not like it.
3 Many artists were not rich or famous in their own lifetimes, but Picasso was both rich and famous when he was alive.
4 The National Gallery in London has a version of Van Gogh's *Sunflowers* on display, while the Philadelphia Museum of Art has another version of Van Gogh's *Sunflowers*.
5 Some graffiti art is sold for a lot of money, although a lot of people don't agree with this fact that graffiti art is sometimes sold for a lot of money.

PART B WRITING TASK

> Should cartoons or comic books be considered art?

3 Write an argumentative essay. Include an introductory paragraph with your thesis; at least two body paragraphs that include evidence in favor of one position, counterargument, and refutation; and a concluding paragraph.

Name: _____   Date: _____

PART A KEY SKILLS
USING YOUR KNOWLEDGE TO PREDICT CONTENT

1 You are going to read an article about the aging population of Japan. Look at the graph and the photo.

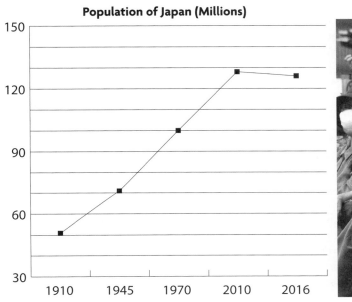

Population of Japan (Millions)

Based on your knowledge of the graph and photo, write *T* next to the statements that are probably true and *F* next to the statements that are probably false.

_____ 1 The population of Japan increased for a century.
_____ 2 Japan experienced a sudden increase in population between 2010 and 2012.
_____ 3 The number of older people in Japan has dramatically decreased in recent years.
_____ 4 Japan is now faced with the problem of an aging population with increased health care needs.

Read the article. Then answer the questions that follow.

The Changing Population of Japan

1   The population of Japan has increased significantly since the beginning of the twentieth century. From a relatively small population of 51 million in 1910, it reached a total of 72 million by 1945. The latter half of the twentieth century saw a huge population boom as the country became fully industrialized. By 1970, the population had surpassed 100 million, almost double its size in 1910, and it went on to grow by an additional 27 million by 2010.

2   In 2016, however, research showed that the overall Japanese population had started to decrease. Except for once, in the year 1945, this was the first time in recent history that this had happened. In 2016, there were one million fewer people living in the country than six years before.

3   A closer look at the statistics reveals that Japanese society is clearly aging, and at a much faster rate than ever before. In 2016, the number of elderly people (people over the age of 65) rose to above 30 million. This meant that elderly people comprised roughly one quarter of the whole population, whereas only 13% were under the age of 14. Japan is now officially one of the "grayest" countries in the world.

4   This trend has been caused, in large part, by Japan's success as a fully developed society. After 1945, Japan, along with many other countries, experienced a "baby boom"—a sudden and dramatic increase in the number of babies born within a short period of time—due to a more stable and economically robust environment. By 2010, these "baby boomers" had begun to leave the workforce. They were officially elderly.

5   An aging society can, in theory, be a positive sign for a society. The standard of living tends to be higher in countries that can support an elderly population. In addition, poverty and crime rates tend to be lower. On the other hand, it can cause serious social problems. For one, elderly people, in general, require more healthcare than young people. If the percentage of the elderly in a society increases, the overall health-care costs for that society will also rise. In addition, as the percentage of younger working citizens decreases, the tax base will shrink. That means that the society will have fewer tax dollars to pay for the costs of health care.

PART B ADDITIONAL SKILLS

2 Put a check next to the five questions answered in the article.

1   What are some recent demographic changes in Japan? ☐
2   What social activities do Japanese senior citizens enjoy? ☐
3   What percentage of Japan's population can be categorized as elderly? ☐
4   Why does Japan now have such a large elderly population? ☐
5   Why do some Japanese baby boomers decide not to retire? ☐
6   Does Japan have a large workforce? ☐
7   In what ways is an aging population a good sign for a society? ☐
8   What are some of the consequences of an aging population? ☐

3 Complete the sentences with the missing information.

1   Between 1910 and _____ , the Japanese population almost doubled.
2   In 2010, Japan's population was approximately _____ million.
3   In 2016, the population had decreased by about _____ million.
4   People are considered elderly when they reach the age of _____ .
5   By 2016, the number of elderly people in Japan reached more than _____ million.

Name: _____   Date: _____

PART A KEY VOCABULARY

1 Complete the text with the correct form of the words in the box.

capacity   demographic   leisure   median   pension   proportion   range

According to our research, the (1) _____ age of the population of Middleville is 48. The (2) _____ of Middleville's population that are considered elderly—that is, people in the age (3) _____ of 55 to 90—is about 20 percent. This is our (4) _____ market, or the people we want as our customers. We have determined that about 53 percent of these people have substantial (5) _____ , mostly from large companies. As a result, most of them have the (6) _____ to spend at least $400,000 on a home. At the same time, they often spend their (7) _____ time actively, which is why our homes are located next golf courses and shopping centers.

2 Complete the sentences with the correct form of the words in the box.

adapt   allocate   cope   document   undertake   voluntary

1 My parents used to love to visit the city, but as they get older, they find it harder to _____ with the traffic and the crowds.
2 Trevor always plans for the future. Every year he _____ 20% of his salary to a retirement fund.
3 As people age, they often find it harder to _____ to changes in their environment.
4 In the coming year, the city plans to _____ the construction of a new senior center.
5 Many senior citizens choose to do _____ activities in their communities, such as tutoring children or helping out in the library.
6 The study published last month _____ the extent at which exercise improved the overall health of the participants.

PART B LANGUAGE DEVELOPMENT
ACADEMIC COLLOCATIONS WITH PREPOSITIONS

3 Complete the sentences with the correct prepositions.
1 The aging population could, _____ theory, cause problems for many countries.
2 The article focuses _____ some of the reasons why life expectancy has improved in the last 50 years.
3 Many young people find it difficult to identify _____ the problems that elderly people have.
4 There are a range _____ theories about why the population has started to decrease.
5 To sum _____ , there are more benefits than drawbacks to having a larger elderly population.

Name: _____   Date: _____

PART A GRAMMAR FOR WRITING
LANGUAGE OF PREDICTION

1 Write sentences with a similar meaning. Include the word in parentheses. More than one answer is possible.

1 People who get good health care will live longer. (likely)

    _____

2 The cost of living will decrease this year. (may)

    _____

3 The average lifespan will be 90 years of age. (predicted)

    _____

4 There will not be a reduction in benefits for the elderly. (unlikely)

    _____

5 The number of retirement communities will rise because of increased demand. (projected)

    _____

FUTURE REAL CONDITIONALS

2 Circle the best verb forms to complete each sentence.

1 If the cost of living *continues / will continue* to rise, we *have to / will have to* move to a more affordable area.
2 As long as my parents *are able / will be able* to take care of themselves, they *live / will live* in their own home.
3 Once they *finish / will finish* work on the new recreation center, we *swim / can swim* there every day.
4 Their home heating costs *remain / will remain* low, provided that the cost of oil *does not / will not* increase substantially.
5 They *offer / will offer* classes in the evening if enough people *express / will express* an interest in taking them.

PART B WRITING TASK

> Describe population trends in South Africa, Mexico, Vietnam, or Italy using data from a graph that you find on the Internet. Discuss the potential impact on the country if current population trends continue.

3 Write an analysis essay. Include an introduction, presentation, and description of the data from the graph. Present at least two challenges related to the data, and a summary of the challenges with at least one advantage.

UNIT 1 READING QUIZ
PART A KEY SKILLS

1 1, 3

2 1 Most people agree that English signs in other countries do not exist for the benefit of tourists.
2 Many researchers now believe that English signs are not intended for English speakers.
3 One possible reason for the use of English in signs around the world is that many people think that English is exotic and fashionable.
4 Many researchers believe that, in fact, English is not replacing other languages culturally in these countries.

PART B ADDITIONAL SKILLS

3 1 F; Japanese is the most common language on signs.
2 T
3 T
4 T
5 F; The Japanese language is not dying out in Tokyo. (The presence of English-language signs shows that the Japanese language is so strong that the Japanese feel comfortable with displaying other languages in addition to their own.)

UNIT 1 LANGUAGE QUIZ
PART A KEY VOCABULARY

1 1 influence 2 situated 3 discounts
4 convenience 5 experimenting 6 relatively
7 authenticity 8 ensures

2 1 fresh 2 insist 3 increases 4 perfectionist
5 consumption 6 selling point 7 specialties
8 ingredients

PART B LANGUAGE DEVELOPMENT

3 1 increased 2 removed 3 confuse 4 exhausted
5 continue

4 1 Obesity 2 multinational 3 diet
4 consumption 5 poverty

UNIT 1 WRITING QUIZ
PART A GRAMMAR FOR WRITING

1 1 sites 2 modern 3 recent 4 new Peruvian
5 a number of

2 1 At the present time, the economy seems to be doing well.

2 Historically, Canada has always been a multilingual country.
3 More and more people have traveled abroad in recently years.
4 Lila Moreno, who was formerly the CEO of PC International, will be the new head of Global Enterprises.
5 We cannot rely on the same systems that we have used in the ~~future~~ past.

PART B WRITING TASK

3 *Answers will vary.*

UNIT 2 READING QUIZ
PART A KEY SKILLS

1 1 DNS
2 T
3 F; Companies want employees with soft skills and certain qualifications, which means that they still care about qualifications.
4 F; In paragraph 4, the writer describes the importance of schools as teaching students practical skills interacting with other people, managing time, and thinking critically. School subjects are not mentioned.
5 DNS

PART B ADDITIONAL SKILLS

2 a 5 b 4 c 3 d 1 e 2

UNIT 2 LANGUAGE QUIZ
PART A KEY VOCABULARY

1 1 core principles 2 evolved 3 online degree
4 concrete 5 launched 6 credible alternative
7 virtual classroom 8 underrepresented

2 1 d 2 g 3 b 4 f 5 a 6 c 7 e

PART B LANGUAGE DEVELOPMENT

3 1 journals 2 plagiarism 3 semesters 4 seminars
5 assignment

4 1 significant 2 motivation 3 establishment
4 principle 5 virtual

UNIT 2 WRITING QUIZ
PART A GRAMMAR FOR WRITING

1 1 In contrast   2 Similarly   3 unlike   4 however
   5 on the other hand

2 *Answers will vary. Possible answers*:
   1 Austin College prepares students for business *while/whereas* Lakeland College prepares them for life. / *While/Whereas* Austin College prepares students for business, Lakeland College prepares them for life.
   2 Both of my parents want me to go to a good school *while* my mother wants me to choose one that is close to home. / *While* both of my parents want me to go to a good school, my mother wants me to choose one that is close to home.
   3 The first two years of college are known for being difficult *whereas/while* the last two are usually very enjoyable. / *While/Whereas* the first two years of college are known for being difficult, the last two are usually very enjoyable.
   4 My science teacher is very serious *while/whereas* my history teacher is very entertaining. / *While/Whereas* my science teacher is very serious, my history teacher is very entertaining.
   5 Diablo Valley is a huge university *whereas/while* City Central is a small college. / *While/Whereas* Diablo Valley is a huge university, City Central is a small college.

PART B WRITING TASK

3 *Answers will vary.*

UNIT 3 READING QUIZ
PART A KEY SKILLS

1 1 infections caused by drug-resistant bacteria
   2 Alexander Fleming in 1929
   3 Doctors prescribe them to people who don't need them or can't be helped by them; farmers add them to food for animals that people then eat.
   4 superinfections; superbugs
   5 tuberculosis; E-coli

PART B ADDITIONAL SKILLS

2 1 a   2 c   3 a   4 b   5 c

UNIT 3 LANGUAGE QUIZ
PART A KEY VOCABULARY

1 1 symptoms   2 conventional   3 surgery
   4 controversial   5 proponent   6 safety net
   7 consultation

2 1 d   2 g   3 c   4 a   5 h   6 f   7 e   8 b

PART B LANGUAGE DEVELOPMENT

3 1 epidemic   2 sedentary lifestyle
   3 preventable illness   4 drug dependency
   5 patent

4 1 b   2 c   3 b   4 a   5 a

UNIT 3 WRITING QUIZ
PART A GRAMMAR FOR WRITING

1 1 an   2 Ø   3 Ø   4 a   5 the

2 1 Despite the fact that / Even though
   2 Nevertheless   3 despite / in spite of
   4 In spite of / Despite
   5 Even though / Despite the fact that

PART B WRITING TASK

3 *Answers will vary.*

UNIT 4 READING QUIZ
PART A KEY SKILLS

1 1 c   2 f   3 e   4 d   5 a

PART B ADDITIONAL SKILLS

2 a 2   b 4   c 3   d 1

3 1 b   2 b   3 a

UNIT 4 LANGUAGE QUIZ
PART A KEY VOCABULARY

1 1 community   2 devastating   3 disrupted
   4 casualties   5 crucial   6 measures   7 rely on
   8 monitor

2 1 identified   2 issue   3 infrastructure
   4 maintenance   5 criticize   6 strategies   7 policy
   8 reduction

PART B LANGUAGE DEVELOPMENT

3 1 a government / governmental report
   2 disaster mitigation   3 risk reduction
   4 flood protection   5 product manufacturing
   6 risk analysis

4 1 a   2 b   3 c   4 c   5 a

UNIT 4 WRITING QUIZ
PART A GRAMMAR FOR WRITING

1 1 It is important to prepare for natural disasters.
   2 It is surprising that more people didn't know about the tsunami.
   3 It is worth remembering that earthquakes can happen at any time.
   4 It is a good idea to prepare for emergencies.
   5 It is a sad fact that so many homes were destroyed in the hurricane.

PART B WRITING TASK

2 *Answers will vary.*

UNIT 5 READING QUIZ
PART A KEY SKILLS

1 1 2 4 6 7

PART B ADDITIONAL SKILLS

2 1 c 2 e 3 f 4 g 5 a 6 b 7 d

3 We ultimately need to find a compromise between preserving existing architecture and developing cities.

UNIT 5 LANGUAGE QUIZ
PART A KEY VOCABULARY

1 1 reputation 2 efficiency 3 relevant
   4 compromise 5 depressing 6 secondhand
   7 durable

2 1 conservation 2 civilized 3 inspiring 4 function
   5 sectors 6 reflect on 7 demonstrate

PART B LANGUAGE DEVELOPMENT

3 1 environmental 2 functional 3 efficiently
   4 depressing 5 responsibly 6 architectural

4 1 b 2 a 3 b 4 a 5 c

UNIT 5 WRITING QUIZ
PART A GRAMMAR FOR WRITING

1 1 critical 2 calculate 3 undoubtedly
   4 significant number 5 Fundamentally 6 justified
   7 approximately 8 have a positive impact on
   9 of no benefit to 10 considerable

PART B WRITING TASK

2 *Answers will vary.*

UNIT 6 READING QUIZ
PART A KEY SKILLS

1 1 c 2 e 3 a 4 d 5 f 6 b

PART B ADDITIONAL SKILLS

2 a 3 b 5 c 6 d 4 e 2 f 1

3 1 T
   2 F; A large amount of power could be generated by enough foot traffic.
   3 F; Piezoelectric floors in Shibuya Station and Tokyo Station power the electronic displays in the stations.
   4 DNS
   5 T
   6 DNS

UNIT 6 LANGUAGE QUIZ
PART A KEY VOCABULARY

1 1 addressed 2 urgent 3 offshore 4 generate
   5 aquatic 6 diminished 7 resistant 8 vital

2 1 inexhaustible 2 alarming 3 adopt 4 utilize
   5 instigate 6 initial 7 universal

PART B LANGUAGE DEVELOPMENT

3 1 b 2 a 3 c 4 b 5 a

4 1 diminishing 2 delivered 3 contesting
   4 consulting 5 utilizes

UNIT 6 WRITING QUIZ
PART A GRAMMAR FOR WRITING

1 1 *who* can live without electricity
   2 *that* was hit by the tsunami
   3 *when* I was in college
   4 *where* large numbers of people live
   5 *whose* homes were near the new dam

2 1 The cost of solar panels, <u>which</u> many people think is excessive, is expected to go down in the near future.
   2 Offshore wind turbines, <u>which</u> are generally very large, can produce significant amounts of electricity.
   3 Geothermal energy is energy <u>that/which</u> is generated and stored in the earth.
   4 The famous actor, <u>who</u> just made a new movie, is a big supporter of solar energy.
   5 People <u>who</u> drive old, inefficient cars should have to pay a tax on them.
   6 The wealthy entrepreneur, <u>whose</u> Caribbean island is powered by solar energy, spoke about the advantages of alternative power.

PART B WRITING TASK

3 *Answers will vary.*

UNIT 7 READING QUIZ
PART A KEY SKILLS

1 a 3 b 2 c 1 d 2 e 4 f 3 g 4

PART B ADDITIONAL SKILLS

2 a 3 b 1 c 4 d 2

3 1 F; The word *graffiti* comes from the Italian word
  graffiato.
  2 T
  3 T
  4 DNS
  5 F; The writer feels that graffiti artists only have a
  right to use public property to express themselves if
  their art improves the structures they paint on.

UNIT 7 LANGUAGE QUIZ
PART A KEY VOCABULARY

1 1 contemporary 2 distinction 3 notion
  4 conceptual 5 mechanical 6 banal
  7 significance 8 objective

2 1 aesthetic 2 sophisticated 3 cynical
  4 established 5 analogous 6 perceive
  7 acknowledged

PART B LANGUAGE DEVELOPMENT

3 1 b 2 a 3 b 4 a

4 1 avant-garde 2 monumental 3 lifelike
  4 abstract 5 moving 6 expressive

UNIT 7 WRITING QUIZ
PART A GRAMMAR FOR WRITING

1 1 b 2 c 3 a 4 d 5 e

2 1 Some art is easy to understand, but a lot is not ~~easy to understand~~.
  2 I like abstract art, but my wife does not ~~like it~~.
  3 Many artists were not rich or famous in their own lifetimes, but Picasso was ~~both rich and famous when he was alive~~.
  4 The National Gallery in London has a version of Van Gogh's *Sunflowers* on display, while the Philadelphia Museum of Art has another ~~version of Van Gogh's Sunflowers~~.
  5 Some graffiti art is sold for a lot of money, although a lot of people don't agree with this ~~fact that graffiti art is sometimes sold for a lot of money~~.

PART B WRITING TASK

3 *Answers will vary.*

UNIT 8 READING QUIZ
PART A KEY SKILLS

1 1 T 2 F 3 F 4 T

PART B ADDITIONAL SKILLS

2 1, 3, 4, 7, 8

3 1 1970 2 127 3 1 4 65 5 30

UNIT 8 LANGUAGE QUIZ
PART A KEY VOCABULARY

1 1 median 2 proportion 3 range 4 demographic
  5 pensions 6 capacity 7 leisure

2 1 cope 2 allocates 3 adapt 4 undertake
  5 voluntary 6 documented / documents

PART B LANGUAGE DEVELOPMENT

3 1 in 2 on 3 with 4 of 5 up

UNIT 8 WRITING QUIZ
PART A GRAMMAR FOR WRITING

1 *Answers will vary. Possible answers*:
  1 People who get good health care <u>are likely to</u> ~~will~~ live longer.
  2 The cost of living <u>may</u> ~~will~~ decrease this year.
  3 The average lifespan <u>is predicted to</u> ~~will~~ be 90 years of age.
  4 ~~There will not~~ <u>It is unlikely that there will</u> be a reduction in benefits for the elderly.
  5 The number of retirement communities <u>is projected to</u> ~~will~~ rise because of increased demand.

2 1 continues; will have to 2 are able; will live
  3 finish; can swim 4 will remain; does not
  5 will offer; express

PART B WRITING TASK

3 *Answers will vary.*

CREDITS

The authors and publishers acknowledge the following sources of copyright material and are grateful for the permissions granted. While every effort has been made, it has not always been possible to identify the sources of all the material used, or to trace all copyright holders. If any omissions are brought to our notice, we will be happy to include the appropriate acknowledgements on reprinting and in the next update to the digital edition, as applicable.

Photo credits
p. 77: Yoshikazu Tsuno/AFP/Getty Images.

Front cover photographs by (woman) IZO/Shutterstock and (BG) f11photo/Shutterstock.

Corpus
Development of this publication has made use of the Cambridge English Corpus (CEC). The CEC is a multi-billion word computer database of contemporary spoken and written English. It includes British English, American English, and other varieties of English. It also includes the Cambridge Learner Corpus, developed in collaboration with the University of Cambridge ESOL Examinations. Cambridge University Press has built up the CEC to provide evidence about language use that helps to produce better language teaching materials

Cambridge Dictionaries
Cambridge dictionaries are the world's most widely used dictionaries for learners of English. The dictionaries are available in print and online at dictionary.cambridge.org. Copyright © Cambridge University Press, reproduced with permission.

Typeset by emc design ltd